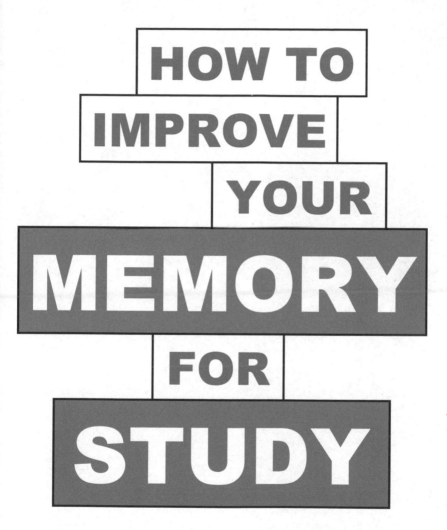

HOW TO IMPROVE YOUR MEMORY FOR STUDY

HOW TO IMPROVE YOUR MEMORY FOR STUDY

JONATHAN HANCOCK

ALWAYS LEARNING

PEARSON

Harlow, England • London • New York • Boston • San Francisco • Toronto • Sydney
Auckland • Singapore • Hong Kong • Tokyo • Seoul • Taipei • New Delhi
Cape Town • Sao Paulo • Mexico City • Madrid • Amsterdam • Munich • Paris • Milan

Pearson Education Limited
Edinburgh Gate
Harlow
Essex CM20 2JE
England

and Associated Companies throughout the world

Visit us on the World Wide Web at:
www.pearson.com/uk

First published 2012

ISBN 978-0-273-75005-5

British Library Cataloguing-in-Publication Data
A catalogue record for this book is available from the British Library

Library of Congress Cataloging-in-Publication Data
A catalog record for this book is available from the Library of Congress

10 9 8 7 6 5 4 3 2 1
15 14 13 12 11

Typeset in 9.5/13pt Interstate Light by 3
Printed and bound in Great Britain by Ashford Colour Press Ltd, Gosport, Hampshire

For Lucy, Noah, Evie and Nate

Smarter Study Skills

Instant answers to your most pressing university skills problems and queries

Are there any secrets to successful study?

The simple answer is 'yes' – there are some essential skills, tips and techniques that can help you to improve your performance and success in all areas of your university studies.

These handy, easy-to-use guides to the most common areas where most students need help, provide accessible, straightforward practical tips and instant solutions that provide you with the tools and techniques that will enable you to improve your performance and get better results – and better grades!

Each book in the series allows you to assess and address a particular set of skills and strategies, in crucial areas of your studies. Each book then delivers practical, no-nonsense tips, techniques and strategies that will enable you to significantly improve your abilities and performance in time to make a difference.

The books in the series are:

- *How to Write Essays & Assignments*
- *How to Write Dissertations & Project Reports*
- *How to Argue*
- *How to Improve your Maths Skills*
- *How to Use Statistics*
- *How to Succeed in Exams & Assessments*
- *How to Improve your Memory for Study*

For a complete handbook covering all of these study skills and more:

- *The Study Skills Book*

Get smart, get a head start!

Contents

Foreword

We live in a world that is increasingly dependent on our ability to acquire new knowledge. The demands on our learning and memory capacities are particularly great during the years of education, when the need to pass exams plays a crucial role in future opportunities. Fortunately, we know a good deal about how memory works. We know that simply slogging away and then racking your brains is one of the worst ways of using your study time, and learning can potentially be both enjoyable and effective. This book tells you how. The author is both an expert in remembering and an experienced and talented teacher who uses what we know from both the science and the practice of memory to help you in the all-important issues involved in preparing for your exams.

Professor Alan Baddeley
Department of Psychology, University of York

Preface

This book will change your life. It may be about studying well, getting the most out of your learning and doing brilliantly in exams, but the potential benefits go way beyond that – because it's also about the way you use your brain full stop.

Training your memory means organising your thinking, developing your creativity, sharpening your learning skills – and, in the process, raising your expectations about all the things you can achieve. So when you get to grips with your memory, it's not just your approach to study that gets a new lease of life. You start thinking and feeling differently about *everything*.

Forget about having a 'good' or 'bad' memory. Anyone can train their brain to remember everything they need. Easy, practical techniques have been around for centuries and they're perfect for all the challenges you face today. The important thing is to understand where memory fits into the study process and to have a clear picture of how the key principles can be applied to the learning you're doing right now – because, whatever you've heard, memory really is essential, every step of the way.

Too many other books leave memory on the sidelines. If they do include specific strategies for remembering these are usually kept in a self-contained section and treated as optional extras, 'add-ons' to more respected aspects of study like collecting, exploring and explaining information. But the truth is that memory underpins all of these activities – and everything else you need to do to succeed. The memory tools you'll find in this book are integral to the whole study process: enriching your work at every stage, allowing you to go further, to learn more, to engage with your subject matter in new ways and then helping you to retain, communicate and apply it all brilliantly.

So memory training is about much more than just memorising information for exams (although this book will certainly help you to do that and it may be exactly what you need if your next big tests are just around the corner). To be truly successful you need to use every bit of your memory in every area of your studies ... and, when you do, you simply start to do everything better.

- You use memories of the past, and vivid pictures of the future, to set up the best possible frame of mind for study success now. Your memory skills help you control your feelings, stick to your goals and make it through the hardest courses and toughest tests.

- You develop a fast and effective approach to gathering information, from books, the Internet, lectures and from all the people you meet along the way with ideas and advice to offer. Memory techniques help you to choose *what* you want to learn and *how* you want to learn it and then to store it all in a way that's useful, meaningful and lasting.

- You organise your thinking to help you organise your time, your resources, your study partners ... and bring a whole new degree of order and efficiency to your learning. At the same time, the creative part of your brain is being trained to make unpredictable new connections, develop powerful ideas and take you to deeper levels of understanding. You do more, know more, understand more – and add it all to your ever-increasing memory store.

- You prepare for assessments and exams knowing exactly how to lead your own learning: how to set yourself up, in body and mind, for a brilliant performance on the day; and then, when that day comes, how to access and apply everything you've learnt.

- You do all of this by exploring how your memory works, then changing your learning habits to match – whatever type of course you're taking, however your abilities are being put to the test. Discovering how to use your brain at its best lets you take control of the whole study process and start creating rich and powerful memories about everything you need to know.

This book is designed to have some immediate effects, so prepare to feel differently about your studies from the start. There's a long and noble tradition of memory training, but you can reap the rewards from the moment you join in. You'll get more fun and fulfilment from your learning, see some rapid improvements in your results and discover the dramatic difference it makes when your approach to study puts memory skills centre stage.

So be positive, keep an open mind and get ready to transform the way you use your brain. Throughout your studies – throughout your *life* – a strong and confident memory really can be the secret of your success.

Acknowledgements

For their advice and support during the writing of this book, I'd like to thank Katy Robinson, Steve Temblett and all the team at Pearson Education. Martin Toseland and Professor Alan Baddeley helped to get the whole project off the ground and my agent, Caroline Shott, has provided invaluable guidance throughout. Thank you also to everyone at the Learning Skills Foundation and to the many teaching colleagues, friends and family who have shared their ideas and experiences with me – especially my tutors at the universities at Oxford and Brighton and Paul Clingan and the staff of Cardinal Newman Catholic School in Hove.

How to use this book

How to Improve your Memory for Study has been designed to be as practical and useful as possible. You can read it in order from beginning to end or you can go straight to sections that are particularly important to you now.

The book is divided into six parts: a progressive course showing you how to train your memory skills and put them to use in every dimension of your studies. The parts are arranged into chapters, each focusing on a particular area to develop. Read the Introduction at the start of each chapter and check out the Key topics and Key terms to get an idea about what's involved. Each chapter includes practice Exercises and activities; and, at the end, Practical tips to try immediately, along with a set of And now instructions to help you apply these new skills to your real study needs.

Throughout the book, look out for some invaluable Smart tips, many taken from my own experiences as a student, teacher and memory champion. Take every opportunity to give them a go and find out which ones work best for you. There are also Information boxes, explaining particular terms and concepts and Query boxes, which get you thinking about your own experiences, opinions and ideas.

This is a practical training guide, so you'll need to flex your mental muscles and challenge yourself to use your brain differently. Having a good memory is about knowing how to use it, then *using it*; so, get practising, apply the advice, put all the techniques to the test and use this book to change the way you study for ever.

Smart tip boxes emphasise key advice to ensure you adopt a successful approach.

Information boxes provide additional information, such as useful definitions or examples.

Query boxes raise questions for you to consider about your personal approach to the topic.

At the end of each chapter, there's a **Practical tips** section with additional suggestions for action. You should regard this as a menu from which to select the ideas that appeal to you and your learning personality.

Finally, the **And now** box provides three suggestions that you could consider as ideas to take further.

YOUR STUDY BRAIN

1 | What is memory?

Introduction

This chapter explores what memory is and how it works – which is crucial to understand if you're going to succeed in your studies. Examining what happens when lasting memories are made is the first step towards using your brain at its brilliant best.

Key topics

- Why memory affects everything you do
- The power and potential of your brain
- Learning to learn
- Different kinds of memory
- What's special about studying
- How your memories are stored
- Where the memory-making process begins

Key terms

Neurons; synapses; procedural, semantic, episodic, autobiographical and prospective memory; study; hippocampus, cerebellum and amygdala; declarative learning; the 'holographic brain' theory; short-term, long-term and working memory

● Meet your memory

To succeed as a student you need to get to know your memory: the complex set of systems that has such a dramatic influence on everything you do. It's no good writing off your memory as faulty, trying to get by without it, or suddenly deciding to use it the night before your big exam. You need to have a quality, lasting relationship with your memory and it can be your greatest ally – but only if you know what it is, why it's so important and how you can exploit it in every area of your studies.

From the outset you need to have a sense of how phenomenally complicated memory is, but also a clear picture of the very straightforward things you can do to use it to maximum effect.

● Memory is everything

You are the sum of your experiences: without them, you just wouldn't be you. Everything you think, say and do relies on memory.

On the most basic, physical level, your survival depends on an instinctive routine of heartbeats, lung breaths, chemical reactions. Your system remembers to keep you alive. Other things you've learnt to do and now remember without thinking: balancing, walking, using your hands and fingers, carrying out countless tasks and techniques that have become embedded in your memory and happen automatically. You've learnt to use language, in your silent thoughts and out loud, remembering the complex ways in which letters and sounds combine to make words, what things are called and what they mean, and how to use at least one language system to communicate with yourself and others. Language has helped you to build up a rich knowledge of the world: the people, things and places around you, along with all the information you've gathered about life in general and the specific fields you've studied.

Your memory is active every second, coping with the present moment, updating your knowledge as things change, accessing your stores of

ℹ️ Memory power

In your brain you've got around a hundred billion nerve cells, *neurons*, each with around 7,000 connections to others around them. Some aspects of the brain are streamlined and simplified as the years go by, but yours still has as many as 500 trillion *synapses*, the pathways between cells that give you all the physical capacity you need for a lifetime of rich, interconnected memory-making. More than just the most complex bit of you, your brain is the most intricate mechanism of all. It may account for only 2 per cent of your bodyweight but it needs 20 per cent of the oxygen in your blood, so it works hard. The wrinkled, spongy, moist, grey lump between your ears holds 100,000 miles of blood vessels and the electricity it uses could light a 10-watt bulb.

past experiences – and looking into the future to create 'memories' for things that haven't even happened yet. This book is about doing more with your memory, but you need to begin by celebrating its power right now. You've learnt a miraculous amount already, you recall much of it flawlessly and you're constantly adding new information into the intricate, infinite storage system we call memory.

● Memory and learning

Your brain is built to learn. You've already used it to store vast amounts of information about your experiences, using all your senses to create personal memories, teaching yourself about the world and how you can operate in it and gathering detailed knowledge and understanding from a range of sources.

Your first teacher was experience itself, the information gained directly through your senses. Then, as your thinking developed, you learnt to learn in a more abstract way, taking hold of *ideas*, linking new concepts with things you already understood and making sense of the world by forming connections. As your abilities with language improved you were able to access deeper levels of meaning. From simple number skills you made increasingly complex discoveries about maths. Every new learning experience became a building-block for the next. All your life you've gathered details, facts and figures, but you've also discovered the importance of patterns, rules and systems, building your scientific knowledge and understanding, gaining a sense of the bigger picture of history, geography, economics ... of the past, the present and the possibilities ahead ... equipping yourself to cope in any discipline – and adding every new bit of learning into the vast, multi-layered, interconnected collection that is your memory.

Your DNA, your experiences and the ways in which you've used your brain have all contributed to the memory you have today; or, rather, to the *memories* ...

Different types of memory

Procedural memory is remembering how to do things. Once gained, skills can feel like second nature – but getting there can be tough and you need to know how to make the most of all the help you get along the way: how to study, learn, practise and master a range of procedures and techniques.

Semantic memory means your knowledge of the world: vast, but far from perfect. Retrieving key details can be difficult and adding to your mental database is particularly challenging when the information is abstract or fragmented, hard to understand or a struggle to engage with – and that's so often the case with the material you have to study.

Episodic memory is your collection of experiences and events, including personal, *autobiographical* memory. Some moments are much easier to recollect than others and the accuracy of all of them can be questionable to say the least, thanks to the interplay between memory and imagination. But these memories can be intense and powerful and they can be used to remember absolutely anything: equations, dates, languages, quotations, essays, systems … You can imagine yourself into close contact with everything you need to explore, understand and remember. You can combine instinctive memory principles with conscious, controlled learning.

Prospective memory is one of the hardest sorts of memory to control: remembering things that are yet to happen, like appointments, birthdays, jobs to do. It's vital for good organisation, time management and efficient working, so it's a crucial element of successful study.

So what is *study*?

Where does studying fit in with all the ways you've been building your brain since before birth? A collection of different memory skills, it's clearly a very specialised form of thinking and learning, with its own challenges and rewards. Think about the place it occupies in your overall 'education'. Consider all the memory-building that's gone on before you ever thought about studying anything and reflect on the learning experiences that have contributed most to your understanding – of the world and of yourself. As you prepare to take a fresh approach to learning, think about the aspects of your memory that might benefit you most in all the study you do.

● Born to learn

The things you know now are a combination of organic learning and targeted study, which will be true for the rest of your days. You've chosen to read a study-skills book, so it's likely that this current stage of your life is geared towards focused, strategic learning. But you need to explore the way your memory works for *everything*, because the best techniques for studying and exam-taking are simply extensions of core memory principles – the things you've been doing successfully since before you were born, whether you knew what you were doing or not.

More than life-long learning

Experiments have shown that babies in the womb can learn sequences of sounds. They react to music they heard pre-birth and they seem to gel a head-start on counting if they've been played repeated patterns of notes: one beep, two, three ... Our brains are built to spot sequences and to use patterns to structure memories, and it's just one of the many instinctive techniques we can use when we have something very specific to learn.

● Time travel

Try this quick experiment. Think of a powerful memory from your childhood: a particular moment that sticks in your brain. Concentrate on the images you see in your mind's eye, but also consider any other senses that connect you to this piece of the past: maybe the taste of party food, the smell of the countryside, the feel of a piece of clothing, the sound of the ocean ... Then try to describe the moment in words: on paper, out loud or just in your head. When and where did it happen? Who was there? What was going on? More details may spring to mind and you might well be able to connect this memory to others. It's a jigsaw piece in a huge puzzle and, for some reason, this one is still clear in your mind while others have faded. You can't remember every childhood day, so why is this one so clear?

- It's likely that strong feelings helped to create a lasting memory, positive or negative. *I was so excited that morning, but I'll never forget how scared I was when the clowns came on.*

- Sense impressions will have strengthened it and help you to recall the details now. *The smell of cut grass always takes me straight back to that afternoon.*
- Understanding is important, too, even if you haven't got the whole story. *I must have been six, because that was the year we went to France and I'm sure the park where we had our picnic was in Paris ...*

Some of the details may be faulty, especially if you've rehearsed them many times, but it's a powerful recollection of bits, so many interwoven strands, so many chains of connection – and it's important evidence of the way your memory works, when it works well.

To make this memory you took in the moment through your senses – or at least parts of it. Many bits went straight in and out and weren't in reach for long enough to become memories, but some did, were held on to, mixed with other pieces of information and kept alive for the time it took to be stored as memories. You've gone back to them in your mind many times since to embed them (and probably to change them subtly over the years), but these details are still accessible, provoking feelings, delivering facts, inspiring ideas ... and connecting with many of the memories that were made before and since.

? Be a memory detective

Think about a powerful memory from your past, exploring all the details you can remember – then check your accuracy by looking in diaries, finding old photographs and films or talking to other people who were there. Notice the sorts of things that you remember correctly, but also the ways in which even strong personal memories can be faulty. Your imagination plays tricks on you, memories often change as time goes by – and this is really important to know because it's going to be a vital part of your memory training. You'll be learning how to create imaginative memories for anything and everything. You'll find out how to 'trick' your brain into remembering.

Memory: fact or fiction?

Real and imagined experiences can become very blurred in the brain. There's a fine line between what actually occurred and what you invented. Scans have shown that two-thirds of brain activity is the same whether something really happened or not and it's an aspect of memory that has huge implications for study. What if you could learn to *create* powerful memories, with as much impact as real experiences, to help you remember everything you needed to know?

Choose to confuse?

Think of a time when you said, 'I don't know if I dreamt it, but ...' What about the phrase: 'Did I imagine it, or ...? We say these things because we really do get confused between dreams, flights of fancy, imaginative ideas - and real-life events. Consider how similar these memories can seem. Have you ever thought about making the most of this confusion: designing memories specifically to support your studies?

When you want to make your memory work - in particular, when you're researching, studying and revising - you can tap into your most powerful, most natural memory-making processes. When you know how to turn anything into a lasting memory you can add in all the strategies for keeping memories alive, connecting them to others, retrieving and applying them whenever you want ... and you have a powerful approach that can be turned to any learning challenge.

So what has to happen for an experience to become a memory? Not everything makes it to long-term storage, so how do you start choosing what you want to remember?

In search of memory

For centuries, scientists have been hoping to 'find' memories stored away somewhere in the brain and to discover the precise processes that got them there. Unfortunately, it hasn't proved to be quite as simple as that. The more closely we explore it, the more complicated the human brain appears. It's possible to lose whole sections of your brain and still be able to think and learn. Some mental functions are clearly located in particular areas, but individual memories can be spread to different places and even simple thinking tasks involve activity across the brain.

Mapping the mind

It seems that our memories are formed and stored all over the outermost layer of the brain, the cerebral cortex. The four lobes have their own specialties: the frontal lobes, for example, are vital for short-term learning and the coordination of memories, retrieving details from the past and making plans for the future; and autobiographical memory relies strongly on the temporal lobes. Beneath the cortex ...

- the *hippocampus* transfers memories from short- to long-term status and it's vital for 'declarative' learning – information you can communicate – and for memories involving shape and space

- the *cerebellum* is involved in storing procedural memories and motor skills: robust learning that's accessible without conscious thought

- the *amygdala* is central to remembering and processing emotions and plays a key role in laying down long-term memories.

Holographic memory

Imagine a hologram: one of those three-dimensional images captured on a two-dimensional surface. If a hologram is broken into pieces, each bit still holds the original image, just a smaller, weaker version – and this quirk has given rise to a theory called 'the holographic brain'. What if, like a hologram, your brain stores memories everywhere and nowhere in particular? Can you imagine memory as a complex assembly process, rather than just a collection of stored data? Perhaps we should stop looking for individual memories in particular places and start drawing on the connective, collaborative power of the whole brain – celebrating memory as much more than the sum of its parts.

● Survival strategies

Memory is clearly a very complex process. Once stored successfully, memories can last a lifetime in a richly interconnected data store. We're good at taking in information, but what happens next is much less straightforward. You could easily be told a mathematical formula, read the name of a figure from history or watch a construction technique being demonstrated, then lose the information instantly, the details passing in and out of your head and disappearing for ever. In fact, your brain is designed to disregard much of the information it encounters, otherwise your excellent senses would overload it with details that have nothing to do with your survival and success. But, as your own autobiographical memory proves, plenty of things do survive the passing moment and stand the test of time. Understanding why this happens has to be a key step towards studying well.

● Short-term v. long-term memory

Many different things affect how well something is remembered in the long term, such as:

- your commitment to learning
- the importance you place on the subject matter
- how often you study it
- the ways you're able to use it
- the things you do to keep it fresh.

But none of the above means anything if the information doesn't even make it over the first hurdle, doesn't even stay within reach beyond the passing moment.

In memory research, 'short-term' now means very short indeed; and not just a slightly weaker form of long-term memory but a different thing altogether. Information can be held for a few moments, but then lost for good – unless something happens to transfer it into longer-term storage. Simply seeing or hearing something doesn't guarantee that we'll still have access to it even a few seconds later. We all know that from bitter experience, but it doesn't stop many students trying to learn in the most passive ways – and then wondering why so little of it sticks.

The life of a memory

Your sense organs detect details, get them inside your head and then the information is held on a very temporary basis in what we now call 'working memory'. After that, *some* of it gets transferred to more lasting storage, 'long-term' memory, from where it can be accessed for a long time to come: for a lifetime, potentially, if the right things are done to keep it secure.

Using your memory well means understanding how it works in the short and long terms. As the next chapter explains, you need to take control of studying from the very start: from the moment you meet information that you want to explore and remember.

Practical tips for getting to know your memory

Spend some time thinking about the different types of memory: procedural, semantic, episodic, prospective. For each of these headings, pick a particular 'example' memory that comes to mind: learning to ride a bike; all the sporting terms you know; your last holiday; the tutorial you need to go to tomorrow. Consider how these collections of information have been built into your brain, how securely they're fixed, how easy they are to access and how they 'feel' when you bring them to mind.

Choose an event that's happened recently – one that you've had no particular reason to think about since. Then go through your senses one by one (sight, hearing, taste, touch, smell) and see how much each one helps you to access the memory. Start focusing on the way senses activate memories, learn about the ones that will be most useful to you – and highlight the ones you'll need to develop.

As well as your experience of long-term learning, start thinking about your short-term memory skills. Get a friend to read out the following sets of numbers to you. After each burst of information wait ten seconds and then repeat as much of it as you can from memory. What's the longest set that you can learn like this? How long do you think this learning will last? Can you feel yourself doing anything instinctively to hold on to the information?

374

9621

69205

782041

6392045

82983461

083928745

2563647823

90573184937

369281046254

9538263791025

26159273648592

982091678253917

GO And now ...

1.1 **Pick a personal area of expertise, from education, sport, leisure or social life, and think about how well your memory has helped you to absorb vast amounts of information and learn complex skills.** Start noticing and celebrating the power of your memory.

1.2 **Whenever you think about an episode from your past, focus on the many layers of information that make a memory.** Get used to exploring memories from different angles and through a range of senses and begin to understand how one memory triggers many others.

1.3 **Think about your day-to-day studies.** Be honest: how much is your memory helping you and in what ways does it let you down? As you learn more about memory, in all its forms, start spotting the places where it could have the biggest impact on your success.

2 | How memories are made

Introduction

This chapter reveals why some things make the transition from extremely short-term, 'working' memory, into longer-term storage and why others just come and go in the blink of an eye. Neglect this initial stage of the memory-making process and everything else will be extremely tough, even impossible. To do well in your studies you need to access information effectively and then hold on to it long enough for rich, robust memories to be made.

Key topics
- The four stages of memory
- Transferring information from short- to long-term memory
- Your brain's instincts to remember – and forget
- Disruptions to memory-making
- How lasting memories are made

Key terms
Phonological loop, visuo-spatial sketchpad, episodic buffer and central executive; primacy and recency effects; von Restorff effect; chunking; retroactive and proactive interference; active learning

● Memory, step by step

Memory is a complex collection of processes, but it's possible to divide it into four key stages. When you train your memory you learn to do four things well:

- **gathering:** being able to focus, concentrate and use your senses accurately as you collect the information you want to remember
- **holding:** retaining important material for the time it takes to start committing it to long-term memory

- **storing:** fixing the details in your brain in a useful and lasting way, then strengthening and protecting them so that they're ready to be accessed and applied
- **retrieving:** when the time comes, knowing how to rediscover the information you need.

Your studies will hit a brick wall if the first stage, *gathering*, doesn't happen as it should. Too many students waste far too much time trying to learn in ways that simply don't engage their memories, attempting to move forward while their mental gearbox is still in neutral. You can sample any amount of information, but how do you prevent it from simply going in one ear and out the other?

● Working memory

The sense information you take in stays at the level we now call working memory just long enough to stand a chance of being remembered. During this time, different memory processes can kick in to start preparing *some* of it to be retained for the long term. It's a crucial period for your memory and highly significant for studying. If valuable information is lost now, recovering it will be beyond even the capacity of your brilliant brain.

To help you, working memory involves some important systems that can keep new information within reach, for a while.

● The phonological loop

Sounds enter your brain, or concepts are heard in your 'mind's ear', and repetition helps to keep them in your consciousness – otherwise the memory traces quickly disappear.

Juggling sounds

Think about a typical test of working memory: when you hear a phone number on the radio or from across a crowded room. As you look around for a pen and paper, are you repeating the digits to yourself, perhaps even giving them a particular rhythm in your head as you struggle to keep them echoing in your phonological loop?

● The visuo-spatial sketchpad

This is the part of your working memory that holds images: shape, space, colour, movement. Like the phonological loop, information stored here fades quickly, although commitment and concentration can slow down the decay.

? Eyes on the prize

As your tutor displays a detailed diagram, think about how you try to hold the image in front of your mind's eye while you find somewhere to make a sketch. How long can you keep the information on your visuo-spatial sketchpad before having to look back at the screen?

● The episodic buffer

Your working memory responds to words that come together as sentences or sights and sounds structured into scenes and stories. This is your episodic buffer: the system that allows you to connect different types of sense information and store them as sequences - up to a point.

? In working order?

Consider the last play you watched, film you studied or demonstration you observed as part of your course. Think about the sequences - sentences, action scenes, practical procedures - that must have been held by your episodic buffer. What were the limits of this kind of memory, when even a clear structure wasn't enough to keep the information in your head?

● The central executive

These three 'slave' systems of working memory are coordinated by something called the *central executive*, which makes decisions about switching between strategies and pays attention to particular sorts of information. When you start thinking about how your own short-term memory works, you quickly realise that there are a number of important factors affecting what gets remembered and what's left behind.

● Test your memory

Here's a classic test in short-term memory, revealing some very significant points about your brain in general and your studies in particular – especially the early stages when you're gathering and trying to hold on to information to learn. To get the most out of the exercise, try to turn off any learning strategies and just listen to the following words as someone reads them to you aloud. See what your memory does when you simply present it with a collection of random words.

hat   tree   glass   cake   leaflet   cockatoo   football   boot
parrot   quiet   apple   riot   coin   hobnob   budgerigar
tired   coat   line   Sherlock   Holmes   bookcase   firework
cockatiel   cloud   horse   walk   shell   tie   doll   teacher

If you'd stored these words in a computer file, as long as the hardware and software were working properly, the information would have stayed put, but human memory is different. Each item in this list is not necessarily as memorable as the next. Learning and recalling is a much less stable and predictable process – although there are some key principles that can be observed.

Start by recalling as many of the words as you can, reading them back to your friend to check off or just writing them down yourself. See whether your results match the following typical trends.

● The primacy effect

It's easier to remember material at the start of a learning period, when your energy and attention are high and the information doesn't blur with anything that came before. Did you recall words like *hat*, *tree*, *glass* and *cake*?

● The recency effect

At the end of a study session like this your memory skills peak again. You don't have long to retain the details before answering and no new words arrive to disrupt the ones you're holding in your head. You may well have remembered *teacher*, *doll*, *tie* and *shell*.

● The von Restorff effect

It's easier to remember information that's unusual in some way and stands out from the rest. The German psychologist and physician Hedwig von Restorff pointed out that strangeness, originality, humour, surprise – and any qualities that get your attention and separate something from the things around it – will make it intrinsically easier to remember. In the list you heard, *Sherlock Holmes* stood out - two words but one idea that was clearly different and memorable.

Like a sore thumb?

Look back at the other words you remembered. Which ones were unusual in some way? When you remind yourself of the ones you forgot, were they the plain, abstract colourless words - like *leaflet*, *tired* and *walk*?

Weird is wonderful

Start using the von Restorff effect in your studies today. Add unusual features to your notes, highlighting key details in ways that will make them stick in your memory. When the information provokes a reaction from you - surprise, squeamishness, excitement - exaggerate the feeling. Add bright colours, bizarre doodles, surprising fonts: not to everything, but just enough to make the really important points stand out.

Whatever works

Think about how your working memory might have helped you in this task. Were the last few words still held in your phonological loop? Did particular words 'echo' easily in your mind - like *cockatoo* or *hobnob*? Which words inspired images to go on your visuo-spatial sketchpad: maybe *riot* or *firework*? Was your episodic buffer helpful for connecting ideas, like *football* and *boot*? Did your brain spot the group of linked words - the *cockatoo*, *parrot*, *budgerigar* and *cockatiel* - or even start to create sequences and structures of its own: maybe getting the *cockatiel* to fly out of the *cloud* or the *horse* to *walk* on the *shell*?

Bite-size bits

Your brain patterns and 'chunks' information instinctively, but you can also start to do it consciously: learning play characters in pairs, for example, or arranging your science vocabulary into themed groups of words. Organising your study material carefully can make it much easier on your memory (see Chapter 5).

● Instantly forgettable

Experimenting with your memory like this should reveal why some of your learning is less than successful. One of the major challenges of study is that much of the material you're given to explore is extremely forgettable, at least when you receive it: black and white words on a page, resources that look identical, abstract concepts, unconnected ideas. If you're just reading or listening, your natural memory systems will do their best but they're going to struggle. Your brain is very different from a computer and just inputting the information is not enough to keep it all there.

Other things get in the way of your memory. Lack of attention, low motivation, no rehearsal ... These and other negative factors might have made the words test even harder and the same happens during many students' day-to-day efforts to learn. It's important to be aware of all the early challenges to your memory, otherwise your studies will never get past square one.

Interference

In these first stages of the memory process, while information is being held loosely, your brain is easily distracted. Memory researchers talk about interference, *proactive* and *retroactive*.

Proactive interference: when material you've seen previously confuses you about the new information you're trying to learn.

Retroactive interference: a new set of data confusing you about the similar things you've just seen.

So a list of chemical elements, say, would be harder to learn if you'd just seen a different but similar list (proactive interference) or if you were presented with another one straight afterwards (retroactive interference) – or indeed if any kind of activity distracted your brain before longer-term memories could be made.

A change is as good as a rest

Help to defeat interference by organising your study-time carefully. Be aware of trying to learn too many similar sets of information back-to-back. Switch subjects and topics regularly to avoid confusion and to remember more and always be alert to the distractions that hamper your memory.

From the moment you're presented with information to study there are barriers to taking it on board. Don't despair: recognising the difficulties is a vital step to dealing with them, and it's possible to take real control of the learning process right from the start.

Getting to know your memory means exploring its strengths and its limitations, then adapting your approach. Successful students know how to create the right conditions and use the best strategies to make everything match the way their brain works best.

Marketing memories

Think about how advertisers activate your memory. An advert broadcast on the radio, splashed across a billboard or shown on a TV or cinema screen can easily wash over you - or its images, puns, sounds, jokes, surprises, emotions and countless other qualities can make it stick in your mind. What if you could start 'advertising' all your study information to yourself, making sure that everything you saw, heard and did fixed itself firmly in your mind?

● Memorable learning

How well you remember something - how accurately, how deeply, how strongly - has a lot to do with how powerfully you experience it, in those vital early moments when the memories are made - or not.

We take in huge amounts of information, but we're wired to be selective. Our brains are alert at certain times. We're always trying to find the information that's important, the things that might have a long-term impact on our understanding, our happiness, and, ultimately, our survival. Short-term memory may keep the sense inputs within reach while more permanent storage can take place, but if the material just isn't memorable then you need to *do* something –

or much of it will be gone for good. Simply sitting through lectures or reading and re-reading notes and textbooks doesn't even come close to delivering the powerful, personal engagement that makes lasting memories.

? Easy come, easy go

In your current studies, which aspects are easiest to forget instantly? Think about the material that doesn't interest or excite you, is hard to understand, gets confused with other things or doesn't even seem important to your ultimate success. If you're going to engage with this information, connect it with other parts of your work and retain it for exams, you're going to have to kick-start your memory and take a new active approach to learning.

● Taking control

Investigating your short-term memory gives some important clues about what your brain needs to be brilliant:

- heightened senses
- internal dialogue
- pictures to work with
- structure and sequence
- reasons to pay attention.

You need to make the most of your brain's natural rhythms, conquer interference and take an active role in the way your memories are made. The strongest students have been doing this since ancient times, putting the right learning conditions in place, giving their brains what they need, turning every kind of study material into something that's memorable enough to be communicated and used in any way required.

In terms of your studies today, the real beauty of this approach is that it applies to everything you do. You can use your brain like this when you're planning your research, attending lectures, watching practical demonstrations, going on trips, making notes, searching the Web ... not just when you sit down to 'revise'. You know how to gather, keep hold of, then remember and use everything that's going to help you succeed.

It's time to activate the full power of your memory and start studying in a way that really works.

⚒ Practical tips for making memories that last

Consider the ways you've tried to take in information in the past. What strategies have you relied on and which ones have worked? When have you felt confident about absorbing information and when has it been a struggle? Start thinking about the conditions that have helped and the techniques that have supported these first stages of learning.

Experiment with different aspects of your working memory. As well as repeating a date to yourself several times to keep it in your head, could you also visualise it on your mental sketchpad? If you're trying to imagine an art technique explained by your friend, could you also repeat their words in your 'mind's ear'? What happens when you draw equations in the air, tap the syllables of technical words with your toe or do anything else that could support your working memory and prepare for the rest of the learning process?

Pick three or four powerful personal memories and think about why they've stuck in your mind. Why did these details stay with you beyond the moments in real time? Was it their impact on your senses, unusual circumstances, the emotions involved, a particular need to remember – or something else that did the trick? Think about the reasons why some moments become long-term memories.

GO And now ...

2.1 Notice your working memory in action. When you're reading (see Chapter 10), listening (Chapter 11), watching or doing, try to be aware of how your brain is taking in the information. Do you talk to yourself as you read? Would you have an image of the basketball's journey before you took the shot? How do you still know the fourth word in this sentence? The more you understand how your brain works, the better you can support it from the start.

2.2 Observe the primacy and recency effects in everyday life. Spot the times when you naturally remember first and last things: first impressions, parting words, the starts and ends of books and films. Get to know the ups and downs of your memory power.

2.3 Treat memory not so much as something you _have_ but as something you _do_. Successful students have the same brains as you: they just know how to use them – and that begins from the moment they take in new information. The memory techniques in this book are active and energetic and they'll put you in control of your learning – so start thinking of your memory as a set of skills to be strengthened and prepare to use it like never before.

3 | Switch on your memory

Introduction

This is where you really begin to take control of your memory – all of it. Your brain has two distinct halves, each specialising in different types of thinking, and you need to use them both – together – to achieve your full potential to learn. Imagination allows you to engage with information on a new level and create strong, lasting memories. You also need to use your senses to enrich your studies, helping you to connect more areas of your brain and achieve powerful, whole-brain learning.

Key topics
- Left- and right-brained thinking
- The goal of global learning
- How to kick-start your imagination
- Using use all your senses to boost your memory

Key terms
Left and right hemispheres; corpus callosum; imagination; global learning; the senses: sight, hearing, touch, taste, smell

● Use your brains

Successful study demands that you use all the memory power at your disposal. That doesn't just mean trying harder. It's about doing thing differently: achieving a new level of learning by honing your thinking skills and changing the way you operate your brain – or *brains*. The electrochemical mechanism between your ears may be one organ, but its two halves are different – maybe even brains in themselves – and their unique characteristics need to be understood and used to the full. Then the most important moment for your memory comes when the two sides are brought together and used as one. That's when you activate your true ability to learn and remember.

● The science behind the memory art

Neuroscience has helped to explain why classic memory techniques work so well. Modern brain-imaging tools reveal that study systems developed thousands of years ago are perfectly suited to the way our memories are made – thanks to the two-sided set-up of the human brain. Memory may be a combination of processes happening all over the brain, but the two cerebral hemispheres seem to have very specific roles to play.

? Which side are you on?

What do 'left brain' and 'right brain' mean to you? Have you ever described your thinking in these terms? You may even have taken tests to discover your brain 'dominance'. Consider your feelings towards these ideas. Have you been led to believe that one is more useful or attractive than the other? You're about to discover what's really going on between the two sides of your brain and why they're both essential elements of successful memory – but take a moment to reflect on what you *think* you know about the two sides of the brain and how *your* brain is set up.

i Split brain research

Back in the 1960s, American neurobiologist Roger Sperry and his team experimented on patients whose brains were physically split, having undergone an epilepsy treatment in which the *corpus callosum*, the connector between the two hemispheres, had been cut. He was able to test the two sides individually and discover what they could and couldn't do, confirming some 'specialisms' – that the left side was the centre for analytical thought, for example, and the right in charge of spatial perception – but also showing that many activities required both sides at once. In the brains of Sperry's patients, information that would normally be shared between the hemispheres simply couldn't get through. The two halves could operate practically independently –

two separate brains, learning different things, even having their own opinions - but each side was unaware of what was happening in the other and the problems came during tasks that required input from both. It just wasn't as simple as saying that a skill like 'maths' was processed on one side or 'language' on the other. All the important areas of thought required key skills from both sides, in combination.

Left and right

The *left brain* is very good at analysis, organisation, definition. In maths it specialises in exact calculations, precise comparisons and logical problem-solving. To language it gives structure, through grammar and syntax, and provides the definitions of words and phrases. Left-brained thinking focuses on order, linear connections and logical ideas.

The *right brain* helps to find general patterns in maths, to check approximate answers and to handle problems involving shape and space. It supports language pronunciation, offers emotional responses to information read and heard and helps to explore the subtleties and multiple meanings of words and ideas. It is the centre for visual imagery and illogical, intuitive thought.

Global thinking

To be an effective thinker and learner you need to have both sides of your brain working well - and working together. The left brain holds the details, but those don't mean much without the right brain's view of the bigger picture. Your right brain can handle faces, but what's the point if it can't connect with your left brain's capability with names? Everything on one side is balanced and supported by something on the other. Left-brained logic is enriched by right-brained intuition. As Roger Sperry discovered, even the most artistic abilities, while essentially right-brained, rely heavily on left-brained skills. To activate your memory for study you need to switch on the whole of your brain.

No excuses

So resist the temptation to label yourself as either 'left-' or 'right-brained' and don't fall into the trap of seeing one side as more appealing or valuable than the other. Our individual characters may well make us more inclined to particular styles of thinking, but, at our best – especially when we're *learning* at our best – we're always using both sides of our brains.

● Whole-brained memory

All the best memory methods involve both sides of the brain working together. You create vivid mental images to remind you of everything you need to know, then you make them memorable; make them suit the way your brain works. Imagery is a more right-brained activity and you also use that hemisphere to add extra sensory details and a rich layer of emotion. You let your imagination run wild, exaggerating all the image clues, having fun, taking risks, making everything as surreal and surprising as you can.

Then … you use left-brained logic to organise it all and fix it in place in your mind. Structured thinking allows you to link the images into scenes and stories – even arrange them around detailed mental maps – and to learn everything in a safe and strategic way.

When the time comes to recall what you memorised, you know exactly where to go in your mind to find the key information. You can remember it with accuracy, can organise it, calculate with it, compare it efficiently to other material and use your left brain to the full. But … you can also engage with it emotionally, find new connections and deeper meanings and use it fully – because you can see the overall shape of it, grasp the big ideas.

● Imagination is the key

For many learners, imagination is the missing link. Once, it was crucial to the way they played, listened, read and absorbed information; but gradually it has become less important, to the point where it has a very small role in their learning. Perhaps it now seems childish, irrelevant to the very real things they need to study today. The way they're taught, the course materials they receive, the general attitude of their place of study: how much do these prioritise or support imagination? The typical university textbook or lecture handout doesn't have much in common with an engaging, absorbing, imaginative children's book. The subject matter itself may well be extremely creative and inspiring, but that's not immediately apparent; and so studying it well and learning it effectively can be hard if *your* imagination is missing.

When you make imagination part of your study you use both sides of your brain: pictures and stories, chaos and logic, adventurous experiments and real, useful results. The Ancient Greeks and Romans celebrated it, it was very clear to Renaissance scholars and now you need to know that imagination is the secret to mastering your memory.

● Kick-start your memory

Believe it or not, you already have a fantastic imagination. Every night you dream richly surreal dreams and every day you show off your artistic talents, find imaginative answers to complex puzzles, lose yourself in books, see the humour in ludicrous jokes, visualise the possibilities of the future. You picture the scenarios that fellow students describe in class, manipulate images while discussing intricate issues over the phone, make all the scenery for radio plays … your imagination works brilliantly without any conscious thought. But what about switching on your imagination at will, and using it in your learning – especially when the subject matter seems to demand a much more straightforward, conservative approach? Are you ready to put imagination at the heart of your study?

● Sensing success

The following practical exercises start with your visual imagination, your ability to project vivid mental pictures, but they quickly extend to incorporate all the other senses. Just like a powerful dream or intense novel, the imagery you create in your mind can activate sounds, textures, smells and tastes. The more of these layers you can build into your imaginative constructs, the more memorable they will be. You'll be learning in a deeply engaging and lasting way, helping you to explore, understand and connect the information as well as to remember it.

● Seeing is believing

This first exercise focuses on the sense of sight.

Here are eight important tasks to remember: eight things you need to get done in the coming week. This is your subject matter as you practise imagining powerful pictures to represent the real things you need to know.

- Return library books
- Try out for swimming team
- Sign up for tutorial
- Sort out next year's accommodation
- Buy new printer cartridge
- Check student loan statement
- Read chapter on soil types in course textbook
- Buy theatre tickets

Return library books. Design an image to represent this first job on the list. Sometimes the best picture is the first one that comes to mind or you could think how you might illustrate this idea in a children's book or on a computer presentation: perhaps a pile of borrowed books on your desk; the entrance to the library itself; or even the angry librarian, warning you never to be late again. Choose your image carefully, then spend a few seconds focusing on it in your mind's eye.

✔ Take another look

Start by picturing the image from a single, obvious viewpoint, but then see what happens when you change your position. Can you see it from far away and close up, from underneath, round the back – even from within the picture, looking out? Use left-brained thinking to check the details and also take a right-brained view of the whole picture, from every angle you can.

Try out for swimming team. Maybe you picture your swimming costume, the diving boards at the pool or the ripples in the water after you've dived in. Start with the basic image and then add in extra details. Focus on colours, shapes-within-shapes, writing – anything that might strengthen the reminder image in your mind.

Go through the same process with the six other jobs on your list.

Know your own mind

As you choose your pictures and practise holding them in your imagination, think about how easy you find it. Which images come quickly and which are harder to visualise? Do you have most success with objects, people, places, cartoons? Are your strongest images still or moving, big or small, seen from a distance or in extreme close-up? Get to know the way your unique imagination works, so that you can use its natural strengths but also boost any areas of weakness.

As soon as you've invented images for all eight items on the to-do list, see how many of them come straight back to you. Do they return in roughly the right order? Some may be tougher to recall than others, but when you do remember them you can enjoy a feeling of certainty that you're right. There's a sense of 'ownership' of information when you do something imaginative with it – even just turning it into a picture in your head. The pictures appeal to your right brain; and then left-brained thinking lets you link the individual images together and hold them even more securely in your mind. It's global learning in action: a simple story that draws on both sides of your thinking to activate your memory (see Chapter 8).

Perhaps one of the library books topples off the pile ...

- and falls into the swimming pool
- but is then rescued by your tutor
- who makes a protective cover for the book
- out of an old printer cartridge
- which is full of money and spills coins and banknotes on to ...
- the soil-covered floor
- until you block up the holes with old theatre tickets ...

Spend a few moments creating your own memory story and make

sure that you can still see the pictures and know what they mean: the library books to take back, the pool reminding you of the swimming try-outs, the tutor you need to sign up to see ... You should be able to remember all eight items on your list, backwards as well as forwards. You've taken a decision to remember, activated your brain and used imagination to make the information memorable. This is just the beginning. Any list of ideas can be turned into images, explored, organised and then fixed in your memory. Key points could be given visual symbols or seen in bright colours. Details can be deleted, added or updated. Thinking in pictures is a vital early step towards putting your memory under your control.

● Sound advice

Our world is rarely quiet. Sounds have a particular power to change our mood, alert us to danger, help us get to sleep ... and we recognise a multitude of different audible experiences. Sound can be used to enrich visualised pictures, adding a valuable new dimension to all the memories you build.

Here are five chemical elements. Say them to yourself a few times, listen carefully to the way the words sound as you pronounce them normally, then start to experiment, emphasising different syllables, exaggerating particular bits of each word – and all the time listening to the sounds in your head. Use your pronunciation to make the words powerfully memorable, echoing away in your 'mind's ear'.

- Potassium
- Manganese
- Zinc
- Tungsten
- Argon

You could hiss the *ss* of *potassium*; emphasise the 'ee' sound in 'manganeeeeeeeeeese'; bring *zinc* to a hard stop: 'zinC'. Maybe you pronounce the first syllable of *tungsten* so that it rings like a bell, and say *argon* as if you were a pirate.

Echoes of imagination

When you've made the sounds aloud, how easy do you find it to hear them purely in your mind? Test out your general memory for sounds by imagining your mobile phone ring-tone, the voice of a close friend or the noise you make every time you close your front door. Start noticing sounds around you and thinking how you might incorporate them in your learning.

Doing this when you heard a new scientific term would immediately improve your chance of remembering it. Several new words can be blended into a memorable soundscape. Try it with the elements: still pronouncing them in the most engaging ways, but also mixing fluidly from one to the next. Blend the end of *potassium* into the beginning of *manganeese*. Contrast the short, clipped *zinc* with the long, ringing first syllable of *tungsten* ... See if you can use sounds like this to help you remember all five.

Then go back to the to-do list you remembered – the library books, the swimming pool – and see what happens when you enrich the pictures with sound. Can you add an appropriate effect to each idea: the dry rustle of library-book pages, the echoing splash of water in the pool, the sound of your favourite tutor's voice? If you can, you're increasing the number of mental pathways back to the original information and boosting your speed, accuracy and overall chances of success.

● A matter of taste

Remembering tastes helps us to notice when things have gone bad and to re-create the meals that nourish us and give us the most pleasure. Just thinking about a taste can make your mouth water, so strong is the connection between taste and memory – even when it's just a figment of your imagination.

Use this exercise to see how well you can conjure up tastes in your mind and then use them in your learning.

Here are seven countries: the top seven, according to a recent International Monetary Fund list based on Gross Domestic Product.

- USA

- China
- Japan
- Germany
- France
- UK
- Brazil

Pick a piece of food to remind you of each country, then imagine how they would taste: first as individual items, then all mixed together. Perhaps you think about biting into a hamburger for the USA, then a bowl of rice for China, sushi for Japan ... Focus on the similarities and differences between each taste sensation. What if this were a seven-course meal: after the sushi, German sausage, then a piece of French cheese ... Do the tastes help you to remember all seven foods – and the countries they represent?

Practise using your real experiences with food, especially your personal likes and dislikes, to add more impact to the memories you create. Going back to the jobs list, can you bite off a corner of a page in a library book, taste the chemicals in the pool and imagine the taste of the slightly stale biscuits your tutor always serves? See what happens when memories come with tastes attached.

● The magic touch

It's quite a challenge to imagine textures, but it can be done – with powerful benefits for your memory. Touch sensations tap into strong emotions and can alter you mood in a moment: the bathroom floor in winter, a razor-sharp paper cut, the soft fur of your pet cat. In turn, these feelings can add great richness and impact to the memories you choose to create.

Try learning a list of sporting events simply by focusing on texture and touch. For each one of the following decathlon disciplines, pick a detail that you can imagine touching, then bring that sensation to mind as clearly and powerfully as you can.

- Javelin
- Long jump
- Shot put

- High jump
- Pole vault
- Discus

You might imagine the sharp point of the javelin, the scratchy sand in the long-jump pit, the weight of the metal shot ... Choose a different touch sensation for each event, then see if it's helped you to remember.

After that, try adding textures to the to-do list. Run your finger over the embossed text on the cover of the library book, pull your hand through the cool water in the swimming pool ... and work on strengthening each image by exploring it through touch.

● The scent of victory

We all know how powerfully smells connect us to memories. The aroma of a particular perfume, food, chemical or school classroom can instantly take us back decades, triggering all the other senses and tapping into powerful emotions, good and bad. Our ability to recognise some key smells very quickly helps us to stay safe and it's another natural mechanism of the mind that we ought to be weaving in among our other study skills.

Could you learn the colours of the Olympic rings, in the order in which they're linked together, by using your imagination for smells?

- Blue
- Yellow
- Black
- Green
- Red

Try it. For each colour, choose an item that has a distinctive smell. Maybe you go for the savoury–sweet smell of blue cheese; then mouldy banana for yellow; followed by tar, freshly cut grass and finally the scent of a beautiful red rose. As always, doing something, anything, to the original information immediately gives you a better chance of remembering it; but spend a few moments doing even more, firing up both sides of your brain to turn the six colours into a whole-brain memory story. Make sure the visual images are strong, link them together in a way that holds them in your head and use your sense of smell – and all the feelings and emotions it evokes – to add a powerful extra layer to the memories.

? Whatever next?

Did you ever think that the smell of a blue cheese and banana sandwich, dipped in tar, then dried out on the grass and decorated with a single red rose could help you learn? As well as seeing if this strange strategy has worked with this real list, fixing the five bits of information in your memory in the right order, think about what this might mean for the rest of your studies. Which elements of your course material could be turned into lists of key points and learnt in this richly imaginative way? This is probably very different from the approach you've taken in the past, so how do you feel about it? Is it childish, inappropriate, weird, silly – or might it just work?

Finally, add smells to your list of jobs. Each of the six tasks already has a clear image, a sound, touch and taste, so why not add one more layer to stimulate your thinking and activate your memory? See how powerfully you can imagine the musty smell of the library, the chlorine in the water, the aftershave your tutor always wears ...

? Spot the difference

Take a moment to consider how much you've done to your original to-do list. It started out as a set of eight fairly ordinary, forgettable tasks, but it's been transformed into a rich, vibrant, engaging memory store, full of details, sense connections and emotional triggers – and now also organised in a way that gives it the very best chance of sticking in your mind. The way you've learnt it means that it can be explored, adapted, augmented and *remembered*, with real confidence. Your imagination has let you take ownership of the information. Can you see how this sort of brain-training and active learning could play a key role in your current studies, and have an impact on your life as a whole?

⚡ Practical tips for activating your memory

Make images the foundations of your memories. Grab hold of any images given to you, in presentations, on handouts or within the words and phrases used by lecturers, tutors and fellow students. When the images aren't there immediately ... invent them: vivid pictures designed to represent everything you need to know.

As well as sight, start making a conscious effort to include all the other senses in your learning. Add vivid details based on sounds, textures, tastes and smells and see how they in turn stimulate a range of memorable emotions. Start engaging more deeply with all the subjects you study.

While you keep strengthening the details, make sure you can also see the 'big picture'. You'll activate even more of your brain if you understand the purpose, structure and wider significance of the things you need to know.

(GO) And now ...

3.1 **Choose five words or phrases from your course that you regularly confuse, misuse or forget.** Consider what they all mean, exactly; design a clear image for each one; then see where your imagination might put them for maximum, memory-jogging effect (see Chapter 14).

3.2 **Pick a distinct part of your studies** – maybe a moment in history, a particular painting or an important political theory – and explore it through a sense you wouldn't normally associate with that kind of information. Spend a few seconds flexing your mental muscles and thinking about the sounds of the battlefield, the taste of the paints, the skin textures of famous political figures. Start using your imagination to explore your studies in surprising and memorable ways.

3.3 **Write up a real jobs list:** a set of things you want to accomplish in the coming week, month or university term. See how well you can create an imaginative image for each item; incorporate additional senses; organise everything so that it's held firmly in your memory; and make sure you enjoy having this list at your fingertips (see Chapter 14).

4 | The right frame of mind

Introduction

The way you feel about your memory has a big impact on the way you use your memory. It influences the goals you set and the work you put in, but it also affects your actual ability to think, learn and remember. In this chapter you'll analyse your current attitudes to memory, explore why you feel the way you do about different aspects of your learning and start to improve your approach so that you can use your brain at its very best.

Key topics

● The connection between mindset and memory
● How your life has shaped your learning
● Different learning styles
● Personal blocks to memory – and how to remove them
● Using different states of mind to boost memory
● Adopting an attitude of excellence

Key terms
Visual, auditory and kinaesthetic learning styles; endorphins; dopamine; acetylcholine; memory capacity; brainwaves; electroencephalogram; alpha, beta and theta waves; mantras; brain plasticity; virtuous circle

● Focus on feelings

To improve your memory you need to explore the way you feel about it. Studying is an emotional challenge, forcing you to leave your comfort zone, face your fears, battle through adversity, perform under pressure – and the way you view your learning skills is a key factor in how well you cope. It helps to determine the amount of effort you put in, where you focus your energies, what sort of practical approach you take, how you deal with difficult moments, whether or not you stay the course ... and, throughout, how well your brain works.

Negative feelings simply get in the way of learning; but if you can get your attitude right, everything else will start falling into place. You need to believe in your memory, because that fundamentally changes the way it operates. The good news is that you can take control of your mindset for study, whatever you've thought and felt about your memory so far.

Analyse this

So how do you really feel about your memory skills now? Spend some time focusing on your attitudes to learning, developed from all your experiences up to this point.

- On a day-to-day basis, how confident do you feel about remembering the information you need to get by?
- For special challenges, like speeches or job interviews, how much can you rely on your memory skills?
- When it comes to studying, do you have confidence in your ability to learn well?
- Do you enjoy the process of using your memory to amass knowledge and skills and show off what you know?
- Do you battle against negative feelings: worries about how hard it's going to be, that it's boring, time-consuming, stressful ...?

Be honest. How much of your mental energies are taken up with fears of failure and crises of confidence: nagging doubts that you'll ever learn enough and remember it when the pressure's on?

Talk it through

You can get some very useful evidence about your attitudes to memory by listening carefully to the things you say - to others and to yourself.

- When you're challenged to learn something - a chapter from the textbook, a complex formula, a practical skill - what sorts of conversations do you have with other students? Do you communicate excitement at the prospect, talk about how you're going to achieve the goal – or do you tell the others how difficult it's going to be and discuss all the reasons why you're going to struggle: no time, too hard, boring, terrible memory ...?

● Waiting to go into an exam, what do you say to the people around you? That you've studied well and are ready to show off or you haven't done enough and you're going to fail? (See Chapter 15).

● What sort of inner dialogues do you have about your memory skills? You talk to yourself all the time, often repeating the same messages, maybe 50,000 thoughts a day – and you can learn a lot by listening.

? Grown-up thinking

It's worth considering how your approach to learning has changed over the years. There's a clear parallel between your maturing memory and the two sides of your brain (see Chapter 3). Children tend to gather knowledge and skills fearlessly, exploring the world through their senses, making instinctive connections, being adventurous, practical and having fun: the very essence of 'right-brained' learning. But adults usually lean much more towards the left: logical, black-and-white theories rather than real experiences, 'serious' learning designed to achieve results. Can you pinpoint a time when the balance shifted in your own learning? The most powerful approach, global learning, is a combination of child and adult, right and left. If you could support a child's instinct and energy with an adult's organisation and efficiency, learn through practice and theory, link pictures to ideas, balance fun with function ... think what that could do for your study success.

Even if you feel confident about some areas of your learning, your overall opinions about memory can be very limiting. Everything you do relies on memory, so the confidence you have in your memory skills is bound to affect all the targets you set and the energy you expend. Henry Ford once said, 'Whether you think you can or whether you think you can't, you're right' and it's an idea that has special relevance to memory. It's all too easy to 'pigeon-hole' yourself as a particular sort of learner, with fixed abilities and deficits, and never come close to your full potential to study and learn.

● Learning styles

Like the terms 'left-' and 'right-brained', particular learning 'styles' are now often used to label people – and, inadvertently, to build barriers to their learning. The different styles can be linked to different stages of life, different personality types, different jobs; and so, even though they all have a role to play in study and should be combined into a powerful joint attack on learning, they become 'loaded' and have some very unhelpful labels attached.

Kinaesthetic learning means learning by *doing*: touching, building, making physical actions. This is typically the approach of young children, with their sensory exploration of the world around them, their touchy-feely books, their action songs – but throughout our lives we experiment with new gadgets, master sports, crafts, scientific techniques and other physical skills and continually use our bodies to learn.

Auditory learning is learning by *listening*: to the spoken word, musical sounds and rhythms – even the self-talk we use to repeat and reinforce ideas in our heads. We rely on this style of learning before we can read, but we keep using it throughout our lives: listening to the radio, talking to friends, sitting in lectures and tutorials (see Chapter 11).

Visual learning involves looking, watching and reading. We watch and copy, then learn from pictures before progressing to the written word. As adults we use maps and diagrams as well as verbal texts and we

Preferences and priorities

Your studies – and your life in general – require you to put all three of these core learning styles to use, but which ones do you feel most comfortable with? Are you naturally more of a kinaesthetic, auditory or visual learner? If you'd just taken delivery of a new computer, would you learn how to use it by experimenting, getting someone to talk you through the instructions or by reading the user guide? Often, you combine all three – but in what proportions? Do the subjects you're studying place particular importance on one style above the others? Have there been times when you've rebelled a little, maybe stepped out of your comfort zone and learnt something in an unconventional way? When have you been able to utilise all three learning styles at once?

achieve a large proportion of our learning this way – reflecting the pre-eminence of sight among our senses (see Chapter 10).

(see Chapter 10)

✔ Open your mind

Once you've considered your right-brain, left-brain balance and thought about your preferred and most-practised learning styles, get ready to get better. Relying on one particular approach narrows many other avenues for study success. You're analysing your current approach to learning so you can extend it, train the bits that are weak and give yourself a set of memory skills to unlock the full power of your brain. Relish the chance to change, to expand your thinking and start studying in new ways.

Nothing about your personality, your interests or your experiences needs to hold back your learning. Everything about you can be turned to your advantage: some aspects strengthened, some developed. But it's all too easy to sabotage your success by clinging on to false beliefs about your abilities or rehearsing moments when you felt your memory let you down …

? Nagging nightmares

When you encounter negative feelings about your memory, can you pin them on particular experiences from the past? Think about how well you've used your memory in tests and exams throughout your education so far and in other challenges like learning to drive, giving a talk from memory or performing for an audience. Can you find 'evidence' of memory being difficult and your own skills being faulty? Are these general patterns of experience or particular moments that stick in your mind – and do they still affect your attitudes to learning? It may be uncomfortable, but it's important to think about the reasons why you might be less than confident about memory, so that you can start to change the way you feel – and change the way you *learn*.

i Memory blockers

Worry, fear, depression and distracted thoughts of all kinds make it much harder to remember. Active, energetic learning is a tall order when your mind is elsewhere and even basic aspects of memory are disrupted when the brain's chemical balance is changed. The brain has evolved to direct its energies as required, but we don't always send it the right signals. It prioritises survival, responding to perceived threat with a fight or flight response and focusing its efforts on immediate need, but that means times of stress can narrow our thought processes and cut off access to the thinking skills and memory stores which don't seem important. So, standing up in class to give a presentation or opening a crucial exam paper, your pumping heart and sweaty palms and feelings of pressure and panic very quickly redirect your brainpower towards basic survival and away from the things you've studied and are now desperately trying to remember.

Chemical assistance

When you're relaxed, memory-enhancing endorphins are released into your brain, improving your mood and helping you to learn. During a stimulating, enjoyable study session, dopamine (another chemical messenger or 'neurotransmitter') triggers pleasurable feelings and rewards you for the way you're using your brain. Acetylcholine is also produced (see Chapter 12) and this seems to play a key role in improving communication between the brain's two hemispheres – which is a vital ingredient in all the memory strategies in this book.

So a happy, relaxed mood helps to keep your memory focused and your brain in balance, but it can be hard enough to find relaxation in daily life, without old memories adding to your stress ...

● Re-shaping the past

If there are specific experiences that are still eating away at your self-belief and hampering your study, memory skills can help you change them, reducing or even removing the power they have over you now. These negative memories have probably been strengthened by repetition and have very likely been exaggerated in the process, so why not use your creative imagination in a more positive way, to alter some of the details in your favour?

Typical moments might be:

- your mind going completely blank in a big exam
- hosting a meeting and forgetting the name of the main guest
- leaving crucial papers behind on a train
- standing on stage with absolutely no idea about your next line.

There are some common feelings in situations like these: stress, fear, embarrassment, panic. Ironically, these are all powerful stimulants to memory. At the time, these primal feelings block access to the types of information you're trying to recall, but afterwards they help to imprint the nightmare moment on your brain.

To regain some control, try the following.

- Take yourself back to the moment in question. If you've thought about it many times since, you probably have a very familiar viewpoint: looking at the exam paper; watching the guest's offended expression; the sight of the train disappearing into the distance; looking at all those faces looking back at you …
- Start with this mental 'camera angle', concentrating on all the details that come to mind – but also try shifting the point of view. Do things look any different if you pull back to see all the other confused students in the exam hall or see the meeting through the eyes of the guest you forgot, who could probably see how distracted you were?
- What if you start re-sizing parts of the memory: increasing the number of people jostling you on the train – *no wonder the papers got lost* – or decreasing the size of you on stage: *your mistake really wasn't as noticeable as it felt.*
- Change the timeframe so that the missing papers are returned in minutes.
- Raise the volume of background noise at the meeting so that your fluffed line was barely heard.

Negative thinking just exaggerates all the bad things, so it's only fair to redress the balance. Use your imagination constructively and start to make peace with the past. Rehearsing these new 'versions' will help you change the way you feel about your memory now.

Memory capacity

You might also be limiting yourself by your understanding of memory itself. It's important to get away from the idea of memory having a finite capacity. We're used to buying computers, disks and USB flashdrives with particular amounts of memory storage, but your brain doesn't work like that. It doesn't store information in the same way, you won't 'fill it up', and all comparisons with computer memory risk blinding you to the true brilliance of your brain. Your learning involves much more than storage. It's about weaving together different sorts of information, exploring it all from various angles, making creative discoveries and achieving deep understanding. You need to think of 'memory capacity' as your *ability* to learn and remember well, not simply how much 'stuff' your brain can hold.

Accentuate the positive

As well as considering the things that make you feel bad about your memory, celebrate the times it works brilliantly. Even people who claim to have the worst memory in the world disprove that dramatically by the knowledge they demonstrate at work, in their interests and just in daily challenges that are taken for granted but are actually phenomenal feats of recall. Dwelling on occasional mistakes can blind you to the awesome power of your mind and to the clear evidence that you can learn and remember vast amounts of information. Allow yourself a moment to reflect on all the things you remember effortlessly; all the times when your memory has worked wonders.

De-cluttering your mind of negative thoughts and ideas frees it up for quality learning and successful study. It helps you to think in ways that support all the different mechanisms of your memory and to make the most of the changing states your brain goes through every day.

Brainwaves

Thinking and learning are electrochemical processes and the movement of energy creates brainwaves – measured in *hertz* on an electroencephalogram (EEG) machine. Studying brainwaves has allowed scientists to see how different mental states affect memory and learning.

Beta is the brain's normal, waking state: 13–25 hertz. The technology around us tends to work at high beta levels and our brains naturally synchronise themselves with their environment – so it can be quite a relief when you turn off your computer and take your brain down a gear. We spend much of our time in the beta state of mind and we can study and learn effectively there, but slowing down our brainwaves opens up even greater potential to learn.

The *alpha* state is relaxed but alert, so particularly well suited to memory. You naturally enter *alpha* as you finish a task, take a relaxing bath or wind down towards sleep; and, even in the midst of study, simple relaxation techniques can help you enjoy the benefits of alpha rhythms. At 8–12 hertz, many aspects of learning are improved, especially connective thinking and creativity. All the whole-brain memory techniques in this book are enriched by alpha-state thinking, combining relaxed creativity with enough attention to stay in control.

Below alpha is *theta*. At 4–8 hertz, this is associated with deep relaxation, often through meditation or hypnosis. Theta rhythms are produced while falling asleep: a highly suggestible time where the imagination is particularly strong. Richly creative connections can be made and long-term memories brought powerfully to mind. It's immersive, imaginative thinking taken to the extreme.

The more you get to grips with your memory, the more you can benefit from all these different brain states. Whole-brained learning trains your logical thinking, so that you organise your ideas, make sensible choices, store information strategically and access it with accuracy; but it also activates your creative brain to get you thinking in pictures, involving your senses and emotions, making unusual connections and finding surprising applications for the things you learn. You can use your memory quickly and efficiently, but you can also take time to explore ideas in depth and explore your imagination like never before. You're always in control of your learning, but, when you want to, you have some new and powerful ways to relax your mind and get even more out of your memory.

● Relaxation zones

Relaxation boosts memory – and the good news is that you can use your memory skills to help you relax. By accessing positive memories and shaping them in your imagination, you hone the visualisation skills that are essential for successful study (see Chapter 5) and you put your brain in the perfect place to learn.

- Choose a location you associate with relaxation. It could be a holiday beach, a meadow on a summer afternoon or just the room in your home where you feel most at ease.

- In your imagination, take yourself to your relaxing place and accentuate all the details: the things you can see, hear, touch, smell and even taste that take you deep into your relaxation zone and remind you of how it feels.

- Enjoy the way your mind can relax your body. Push away all distracted thoughts and celebrate your brain's ability to summon up these positive images and feelings.

Get your brain ready to remember and hone the creative learning skills that will make such a difference to your study.

Memory mantras

Choose a mantra: a positive, affirming phrase that will raise your spirits and help you maintain the best possible frame of mind. It might be something like 'I prove my memory power every day', 'I choose to learn and I succeed' or 'memory is an adventure'. Make the wording as positive as possible and choose phrases that sound good when you repeat them in your mind. The crucial extra step is to attach a memorable image. It's another win-win technique because you're strengthening the mantra and improving your memory. Maybe you see *power*-lines connected to your brain, watch yourself *choose* information books in a library or picture a famous *adventurer*. It makes you think about exactly what you mean and gives you powerful visual triggers to back up your positive thoughts – which have such a profound impact on your memory.

● Expecting success

- Like sports stars, actors or politicians, students need to boost their self-belief, ready to give the performance of their lives.

- The more you believe your efforts are going to pay off, the more motivated you are to put in the time and energy it takes to be great.

- Bear in mind the latest research into the 'plasticity' of the brain: the way you use your brain changes your brain physically, adapting it to work better. Use the memory techniques in this book to practise the best thinking skills and make them second nature.

- Keep focusing on the connection between your efforts and your excellent results and enjoy being in control. Do everything you can to accentuate your positive feelings – because they feed straight back into your memory success.

✔ Target-setting

Set your goals carefully: not too high, not too low. As you get to know your memory, push yourself towards achievements that are aspirational but possible and use your new learning skills to create target images to follow. Visualise yourself answering the exam questions confidently, performing a practical test flawlessly or presenting your assignment to the class. Actually see it in your mind's eye and use both sides of your brain, focusing on the details but also capturing the whole moment. With your left brain, think logically – about why this would be such an important achievement; and with your right, activate your emotions and exaggerate the feelings attached to achieving your goals. Create 'memories' of success as vivid as anything that's really happened to you and use them to keep your spirits up and your focus clear.

✔ Evidence of excellence

Collect examples of your memory at work – and working brilliantly. If you get some positive feedback from your tutor or a thank you email from a friend you've studied with, save it in a laptop file. You could use a document box to store exam certificates or photographs of awards ceremonies. Add to your collection whenever you can and revisit it whenever you need reminding of your memory's power.

Aristotle said: 'We are what we repeatedly do. Excellence, then, is not an act, but a habit.' Habits can take time to change, but even slight shifts in your views about memory can help you to use your brain better. Then you notice evidence that it's working, put in more effort, try new things, find the *right* ways to learn and remember ... and your confidence grows. It's a 'virtuous circle' and it turns faster and faster. Your learning skills improve – and they keep improving – as the best thoughts and behaviours become habits and you adopt the attitude of excellence that will change the way you study for ever.

 Practical tips for getting into the right frame of mind

Be aware of the things you say about your memory. Make gradual adjustments to your 'self-talk' – like changing 'I don't know' to 'I haven't learnt yet' or 'I can't remember' to 'how can I make my memory work?'

Pinpoint any memories that threaten your confidence. Use your imagination to change them, proving to yourself that you're in control of your mind.

Surround yourself with people who inspire you to be positive about your learning. Make sure your conversations reflect your energetic and optimistic approach to memory.

GO And now ...

4.1 **Design your own 'relaxation zone'.** Use your imagination to make it realistic enough to change your feelings and get your brain ready to remember.

4.2 **Choose a positive, inspirational memory mantra.** Analyse exactly what it means and pick a striking image to fix it in your mind.

4.3 **Rehearse future achievements in your imagination.** Create powerful pictures – future 'memories' – of all the study success to come.

WHERE STUDY STARTS

Introduction

This is a very practical chapter, designed to give your memory a workout – ready to get to grips with your studies and achieve new levels of success. It explores four key aspects of memory: a quartet of abilities that you can enrich, improve and then apply to every aspect of your learning. By training your powers of concentration, visualisation, organisation and imagination, you can get all the mechanisms of your memory in gear and prepare your brain for brilliance.

Key topics
- How to improve your concentration
- Learning to visualise anything
- Why you need an organised mind
- Tips for boosting your imagination
- Having fun with your memory and celebrating its power

Key terms
Concentration; visualisation; advertising; organisation; categories; imagination; synaesthesia; humour

● Brain-building

Many qualities and skills contribute to a powerful memory. Improving any of them makes a difference to your learning, but there's no reason why you can't train them *all*, preparing for the full range of memory techniques explored in this book and getting your brain in the perfect place for study.

✔ Just the beginning

None of these skills is new. They're all things that you're doing every day –
but probably not all of them in your studies. The exercises in this chapter
are just examples of the ways in which you can stretch and strengthen
these important abilities. You need to find opportunities in daily life to keep
the training going, but the best exercise comes when you start using them
consciously for study. That's when you feel the effects of them on your
brain and see what a big difference they make to your learning.

● Concentration

Attention is such an important factor in memory (see Chapter 2)
and concentration is your ability to *keep* paying attention: to all the
different types of information coming in through your senses, the
thoughts and feelings they generate, the conscious strategies you use
to process it all, the rest of life going on around you ... It's impossible
to remember a piece of information if you haven't even received it, so
concentration involves staying alert, aware of everything and ready to
spot anything that's useful, but it's also about focusing, homing in on
particular things without being distracted by all the others. To make
the most of your memory you need to be ready for the unexpected
and open to all the information coming your way; but, sometimes, you
also need to shut everything else out and focus all your mental power
in one direction alone, for as long as it takes. That takes practice.

? Concentration levels

Think about your current ability to concentrate on your studies
and the different levels required at different times. What's it like
concentrating on a lecture compared to when you're in a discussion
group or tutorial? How well do you maintain your concentration while
you're watching a practical demonstration, reading a textbook, solving
a complex problem? When you sit down to plan an essay or revise for
a test, how long can you keep concentrating? What times of day do
you concentrate best? Which subjects or activities hold your attention
the longest? What sorts of distractions are most likely to break your
train of thought?

On and off

Get used to being strategic with your concentration. To use your memory efficiently and effectively you need to be able to turn on your powers of concentration and maintain them for as long as necessary, but that also means you can switch them off and relax (see Chapters 4, 12 and 15). Too many students don't know how to make the mental gear-shift between different tasks, so the concentration levels involved in learning aren't very different from those involved in other aspects of daily life. When you've trained your memory you make a very conscious decision to use your brain a certain way, so it feels quite different when you turn on your concentrated thinking and achieve your particular learning goal, then relax: job done. You need to pace yourself, organise your time to vary the intensity, mix periods of intense concentration with more relaxed learning tasks. Don't worry if many aspects of study don't seem to involve concentrated mental effort, as long as the key learning times *do*.

● Concentrating on concentrating

The first step towards better concentration is simply being aware of it: checking if your current level is appropriate for the task at hand and noticing when it changes. If you're tired, hungry, worried, bored, distracted by your surroundings ... ask yourself whether your powers of concentration are good enough or if you're just wasting your time. You might begin a learning session in top form, but gradually feel your concentration dropping and your mind wandering – and that's when you need to decide whether there's any point carrying on. Keep assessing the quality of your concentration.

● How well are you paying attention?

● Are you really reading, seeing or hearing what you should be?

● Are you using all the thinking skills necessary to make your memory work?

● If you're not ... is there still some benefit in letting the information wash over you, to give you a flavour of it for the future – or do you need to stop and do something else?

Concentrated effort

Like a long-distance runner gradually increasing their distances, set yourself targets for how long you're going to concentrate and try to improve your performance bit by bit. If you manage to stay focused right up to the time you set, stop and reward yourself, then extend your target slightly for the next session. Be honest: if you notice your mind wandering and realise that your concentration has lapsed, try to get it back on track – and if you can't, just bring the activity to an end, think about what went wrong and have a go at that same target next time.

● Concentration exercises

Here are some brain-training exercises to help you improve your concentration. Make the most of spare moments. Try them at different times and in different places. How good is your concentration first thing in the morning or in the middle of the night? Can you do these mental activities in silence, with music playing, while watching TV, in a crowded room ...?

Backwards and forwards

Count aloud 'one, two, three ...' and at the same time *visualise* the numbers from ten to one. So you say 'one' while picturing ten, 'two' with the digit nine in your head, and so on. When you get to 'ten'/one, see if you can do the same thing in reverse, counting the numbers down while you visualise them going up. When you're ready, try doing it up to and down from higher numbers: 20, 50, 100 – or more. What happens when you try to carry out the two counts at different speeds? Can you concentrate strongly enough to keep track of them both?

Human clock

Spend a few moments watching the second hand on a clock or the changing numbers on a digital watch. Get comfortable with the length of a second, then see if you can estimate ten seconds. How close to one minute can you come, just by counting the seconds in your head? Try it for longer periods of time and challenge yourself to do it without counting in 'elephants' or 'Mississippis', just by imagining the seconds passing by on a clock or even just listening to the tick, tick, tick in your imagination.

First and last

Have a go at inventing meaningful sentences in which every word starts with the last letter of the previous one, such as these.

- Students should demonstrate excellent technique.
- Learn new ways. Studying gets simpler.

This is a powerful exercise for boosting concentration because you have to think of several things at the same time, continually checking the last letter or the last word at the same time as remembering the developing meaning of the sentence and looking ahead to the first letter of the next word ... It's a good test of logic and creativity and another great way to strengthen the powers of concentration that play such a major role in memory.

● Visualisation

Vital to many memory techniques is the ability to create strong mental images. With practice, anything can be visualised powerfully: given shape, colour, texture, movement and brought to life in the mind's eye. Some things are easier to 'see' than others, but even abstract ideas can be represented with memorable images, then stored on their own, paired with others or incorporated into larger collections of information. It's very natural to think and learn in pictures. Training your memory just means doing it better and using the technique consciously for everything you want to study and learn. The things that don't stay in your memory, or even get in there in the first place, are usually those that don't have any kind of imagery attached.

Picture this

Think about the imagery we naturally insert into speech, to help other people understand what we're saying, to emphasise key ideas and to make the things we're talking about more memorable. We use similes and metaphors (*I was as cool as a cucumber*; *she was a whirlwind*). We turn complex ideas into quirky pictures (*too many cooks spoil the broth*; a *bird in the hand is worth two in the bush*). We compare abstract concepts with striking images; (*I could see light at the end of the tunnel*; *it was out of the frying pan and into the fire*). The most memorable communicators - politicians, performance poets, great teachers - are skilled at making us visualise their ideas.

A good advert for memory

Advertisers need you to remember their messages and they know how important it is for you to have pictures to hold on to. Think about some of the most famous brands. Which images spring to mind? Picture the products themselves, their logos, packaging, company colours; but also see what other pictures the advertising agencies have planted in your memory. Can you visualise moments from TV commercials, key images from billboards, even scenes from radio adverts? Try to analyse the *concepts* that they're making you 'see': things like speed, ease, quality, reliability, fun. To study well you'll need to think like this and start creating vivid mental adverts for even the most abstract ideas.

● Visualisation exercises

Images for anything

In spare moments, practise visualising familiar information: people, places, objects. Bring them to mind in as much detail as possible and explore different viewing angles. Do you naturally visualise them in colour or black and white, moving or still, on the left or right of your mental movie screen? Strengthen your preferred approach but also experiment with less comfortable techniques.

Anagrams

Pick words – the first ones that come to mind or words you spot around you – and rearrange the letters to make new, real words. Explore the anagrams purely in your mind's eye, shuffling the letters around in different combinations until new words emerge. Start with short words (may into *yam*, bush into *hubs*, march into *charm*), then challenge yourself to visualise more and more letters at once. You'll prove that some words don't have any anagrams and that others have several. How many new words can you make by rearranging STOP, DEALS or DANGER? Get friends to jumble up words for you to unscramble. Look at the letters once, then close your eyes and solve the puzzles in your head: YOREMM, NUTSTED, RELSCUTE.

Virtual furniture

You can strengthen your visualisation skills even further by picturing a piece of mental 'furniture', then filling it with images representing a set of real information. You'll boost this key aspect of memory and build a piece of memory 'equipment' that can be used again and again.

Visualise ... an antique oak cabinet. The two doors open smoothly to reveal three drawers on the left, another three on the right and two shelves in between. Create the clearest possible picture of this empty cabinet – then have a go at visualising it *full*.

You could learn this list of weather conditions: perhaps headings in an exam essay or topics to cover in a talk to the class.

snow   rain   wind   lightning   hail   thunder   sunshine   fog

Create a vivid image to represent each word on the list, then put all the images into your cabinet of memories. Maybe there's a snowman in the top drawer on the left, an umbrella in the middle drawer and a windsock at the bottom. Could you visualise lightning flashing across the top shelf, hailstones piled up underneath?

Spend a moment reviewing all eight images, strengthening them and fixing them in place – and then see if you can use them to remember the eight weather words: visual clues inside a visualised memory store.

● Organisation

This is another crucial memory-boosting skill: a very left-brained style of thinking, but one that you can combine with all the powers of your right brain and start using your memory at its very best.

A tidy mind?

How organised is your present approach to memory and learning? Consider the physical evidence: your paper folders and electronic files, bookshelves, bag, desk ... Do they represent an organised approach to study? What about the other clues about your organisational skills: your time-management, prioritising, study/life balance, punctuality? An organised approach, outwardly and inwardly, is absolutely essential to making the most of your memory. It will help you change the way you set up your workspace (see Chapter 13) and handle all your stuff (Chapter 15), but it will also revolutionise the collecting, filing and retrieving that goes on in your head.

Sort it out

Focus on the benefits of getting organised (see Chapter 14). Time spent arranging your materials and equipment *saves* you time searching for missing things. Checking lecture schedules and class timetables ensures you don't miss vital opportunities to learn. When you're organised about what you're learning, you ensure you're learning the right things. Being organised about coursework and exam preparation makes it seem more manageable – it boosts your motivation. It also helps you to understand it, which instantly makes it more memorable, allowing it to slot neatly into effective memory systems, where it *stays* organised.

Sometimes, simply reorganising a set of information lets you learn it with ease. Memorising the letters RMIORYTYOMUDEVUROPOMEYFSR is somewhat easier when you reorganise it: IMPROVE YOUR MEMORY FOR STUDY. This is an extreme example, but your brain is always on the lookout for ways to reshape information to make it easier to hold on to, rearranging and patterning it so that it looks clearer, sounds better or means something memorable. Try grouping the long number 37849320519 into smaller chunks and giving them a patterned rhythm: 378, 493, 20519. Think about the way you might naturally group together drinks or food orders to help you remember them at the bar. You need the confidence to take control of all the information you're given and organise it in the way that best suits your memory.

● Organisation exercises

Letters and numbers

Look carefully at the following sets of information. Have could you reorganise each one to make it easier to remember? Try to spot existing patterns or create your own. Are there better ways to group the individual bits?

a) Learn these letters, in any order: KWQGCYOAESIMU. (Hint: which 13 of the 26 letters of the alphabet are here?)

b) Hold this number sequence in your head so that you can repeat it from memory in one minute: 83418296023. (Hint: rhythm can be a big help.)

c) Memorise these five letter sets: BXO – HTA – PCU – NSU – TPO. (Hint: could you reorganise each group of letters to mean more?)

Intelligent design

When a set of information doesn't have any particular sequence, rearrange it in the way that's most helpful for memory. For example, 'The Five', a famous group of composers in Russia, was made up of:

Balakirev, Cui, Mussorgsky, Rimsky-Korsakov, Borodin

If you were going to invent a phrase or sentence to help you remember them all, you could take the first three letters of each name – Bal, Cui, Mus, Rim, Bor – then organise them in a more memorable way.

You might put Bor and Bal together: BorBal, to sound like 'bauble'. Mus and Rim, MusRim could remind you of 'mushroom'. You could make Cui sound like the call 'Coo-ee' and put that at the start: 'Coo-ee! Bauble! Mushrooom!'

Imagine you're calling for your two dogs, Bauble and Mushroom, who've hidden somewhere. Say these sounds to yourself a couple of times. Remind yourself of the real composers. Then wait a couple of minutes and see if you can use this simplified and reorganised version of the original list to remember the five Russian names.

Categories

Arranging information into sets and categories can help to hold it in your mind. You focus on it, think about it, do something with it – and that can be all it takes to make it memorable. Try it with the following list: a selection of sports and games. Organise them into categories of your choice, lucid and logical or imaginative and surreal. There are ball-games here, water-sports and many other real groups and sets; but maybe there are also 'Mickey Mouse's three favourite sports' or 'Things not to do in the nude'.

basketball, chess, diving, soccer, netball, Monopoly, poker, baseball, waterpolo, tennis, shooting, bridge, archery, badminton, cricket

When you've created your categories, cover the list and see how many of the 15 sports and games you can still remember. Use one sport to trigger memories of others in its set. Think about the groupings that worked particularly well; and, if you forgot anything, consider how it could have been connected to something else on the list and organised more effectively in your mind.

● Imagination

Imagination is the secret ingredient in the memory strategies that will transform the way you study. Once you've visualised the information you need to know and organised it in a way that suits your brain, you let your creativity go to work. You give the images and connections impact in every way possible, make it all eye-catching, funny, strange, surprising – and then arrange it in your mind in the most memorable ways imaginable.

? Risky thinking

How do you feel about entering the unregulated world of your imagination? In your creative mind there are no rules, just a very clear purpose: to make information more memorable. The material you're studying might include extremely logical, practical, serious subjects, but the way you learn it can be richly imaginative and involve only the logic you design. Real details can be learnt in a *surreal* way – and, when you start, that can be something of a leap of faith. Think about areas of your life that already involve imagination – maybe creative writing, theatre, visual art – and enjoy injecting the same spirit into your study (see Chapter 3).

● Imagination exercises

Transformations

Take simple pictures and transform them in your imagination. Think: what's the most memorable thing I could do with this image? You need to retain the original idea, but extend it, enrich it, make it more interesting, engaging, intense. See where your imagination takes you.

wall   hat   rug   flower   bus   cup   shoe

What happens when you change the size of something, to make it huge or tiny? Can you add interesting details, colours, decorations? What if an inanimate object starts to walk, talk, fly …? Use all your powers of imagination to exaggerate something about each of these words. Then, is there something that might link them all together? Imagine … they were all in a giant's pocket or visible from space or picked out in fireworks. Practise operating your imagination strategically – great whole-brained learning – and then see if it's activated your memory. How many of the words can you recall now?

Crossed wires

This exercise pushes you to make some very imaginative cross-connections in your brain: powerful preparation for all the creative memory techniques explored in this book. You need to do more than just know these strategies in theory and this activity promotes the sort of mental flexibility that will take your studies to the next level. The idea is that you learn to ask and answer some very unusual questions. They're questions that feel very strange in your brain because they bring together areas of thought that don't usually meet.

- What colour is fear?
- What does sour sound like?
- What's the texture of a trumpet fanfare?
- How does green taste?
- You can smell coffee, but what shape is that smell?

There are no right or wrong answers to questions like these and, in fact, they usually provoke another question: why? Why do you associate February with purple, happiness with yellow, the number 8 with ice? You might find a vaguely logical explanation for some of your answers, but many of them will be based on forgotten experiences, odd associations

Synaesthesia

This is a condition in which the senses overlap. It's fairly common and many people experience mild effects of synaesthesia: perhaps associating days of the week with specific colours or finding that letters of the alphabet have particular textures in their mind. For a few people, the impact is more extreme. Sounds can have tastes and smells; every word might come with colours and textures attached; and sense information is interwoven to the point of being overwhelming. But synaesthesics report many benefits for their memory, as each bit of information is wrapped in a multitude of stimulating sensory clues. Names are recalled by thinking of their taste or numbers by their smell. You can learn to gain from this style of thinking, too, training your brain to use senses in new ways and consciously entwining them to create powerful, multi-layered memories.

and the strange connections that occur when you explore concepts, senses and emotions in new, challenging ways.

? Have a laugh

Have you ever thought about using humour to help you learn? Comedy is a key component of many memory techniques and you can practise injecting it into your studies. So much of what's funny is unusual, surprising and surreal – all qualities that make things memorable – and the positive, happy feelings generated help put your brain in the best place for learning (see Chapter 4). Spend a moment thinking about how humour connects both sides of your thinking, combining the mundane with the bizarre; abstract ideas with vivid images, predictable patterns with sudden surprises. Many jokes rely on the brand of imaginative mental flexibility that plays such a key role in memory. Think about the cross-brain connections being forged by jokes like these. Why don't cannibals eat clowns? *Because they taste funny.* What's orange and sounds like a parrot? *A carrot.* Two fish in a tank. One says to the other, *how do you drive this thing?*

Comedy script

Practise telling yourself funny stories about the information you want to learn. Use all the stereotypes of comedy, plus the particular things that make you laugh. Imagine your story being filmed and shown to an audience, then hear their laughter in your mind's ear.

Here are ten characters from Shakespeare's plays.

clown, soldier, doctor, gravedigger, nurse,

ghost, shepherd, sailor, servant, cobbler

Maybe the clown skids on a banana skin and knocks over the soldier, who pulls a rude face that makes the doctor think he's having a seizure – and call in the gravedigger. The clown rushes to hide in a cupboard, but finds there's already a nurse hiding in there, trying to escape from Casper the cartoon ghost ...

Use slapstick, farce, satire – anything that gives you a funny and engaging story to replay in your mind. Then see if you can use it to remember all the Shakespearean names on the list – or whatever set of information you've chosen to learn.

Images for anything

Whenever your studies involve an abstract concept, push your imagination to turn it into a vivid, original, memorable image. Build this skill into your brain so that you're confident about engaging with any kind of information, however intangible it seems at the start.

Put your imagination to work on the following five ideas: key terms in a marketing model that describes the interplay between buyer and seller.

attention, interest, desire, action, satisfaction

This is an exercise that combines all four thinking skills explored in this chapter. You'll need to concentrate throughout the task, visualise each idea clearly, organise it carefully – and only then start enriching it in your imagination and making it truly memorable.

Attention could be a bright red warning sign, being scrutinised with great *interest* under a huge microscope by someone whose *desire* is represented by cartoon love-birds, which suddenly spring into *action*, as a movie director also shouts 'Action!' and they start singing the Rolling Stones song about *satisfaction* ...

Celebrate your creativity

To boost your confidence, think about the way your imagination shows what it can do in your dreams, representing thoughts and feelings in richly creative ways.

● Consider how your moods, emotions, questions and concerns can be translated into some very memorable images and events.

● Try to trace the surreal goings-on in dreams to the specific experiences, thoughts or feelings that might have triggered them.

● Think about how your imagination turns the most abstract mental processes into vivid scenes and stories or transforms one train of thought into something strikingly different.

Use this ability to inspire your conscious creativity and to start using it to the full in your studies.

Practical tips for warming up your brain

Learn about the ups and downs of your brainpower. Experiment to find out when you think and learn best and when it's a struggle. Make the most of the times when you're particularly alert, but also work to stretch your learning capacity – even at times when your thinking skills are usually weak (see Chapters 14 and 15).

Practise the skills in this chapter in different aspects of your life. If you can train your concentration while you're playing sports or chatting at a party or expand your imagination during a plane journey or on a country walk, you'll be doing even more to prepare your brain for the challenges of study.

Seize on every opportunity to train your brain: crossword puzzles, chess, Sudoku, video games that challenge your speed, flexibility and bravery of thought. Seek out activities that you find relaxing and fun, but also treat them as an investment in your study success.

(GO) And now ...

5.1 Every day, choose a different mind-stretching exercise – from this chapter or elsewhere in the book. Have it on standby for spare moments or 'dead' time. You'll still have to queue up in the post office or listen to the holding music on the phone, but you can be giving your thinking skills a workout at the same time.

5.2 After every study session, spend a moment considering which aspects of your mental effort had most impact on your memory, good or bad. Monitor the progress of your brain-training, celebrate the things that are working, but also spot the memory-boosting skills that need some extra input.

5.2 Find inspirational examples of the core thinking skills: family members, friends, fellow students, people in the public eye. Who's the most imaginative person you know or the best at concentrating? What clues can you collect about how they got to be so good – and are there ways in which you could copy their approach, as your own brain-building continues?

6 | Strategies for success

Introduction

Successful study demands a very clear plan of action, especially if you're going to get the most out of your memory. This chapter explores the intelligent approach you need to take from the start, to ensure that you maximise your time and effort, learn the right things, make full use of all the knowledge and skills you've gained so far and put your memory to work in the most powerful and productive ways.

Key topics

- Exploring what you *think* you know about the challenge ahead
- How to find out exactly what's required: during the course, as well as at the end
- The importance of organising all your materials
- A practical guide to prioritising different areas of learning
- Assessing what you know, then using it all to kick-start the study process now

Key terms

Assessment criteria; timescale; syllabus; value; traffic-lighting; surface, deep and strategic learning; prior knowledge

● Eyes on the prize

This whole book is about taking control of your memory, but this chapter focuses specifically on the strategic 'plan of attack' that starts it all off. The study process is made up of long- and short-term goals and these need to be at the front of your mind as you make a plan for the way ahead: how you're going to achieve success at each 'end point', but also how your memory skills will help you throughout your course.

Your memory works best under your conscious control, directed and activated to learn quickly, accurately and effectively. You need an overall plan that takes in what you have to learn, by when, to what depth, in what format ... but it also has to include all the different ways that memory can help you hit your targets. It's this detailed and strategic approach that will save you a great deal of time and energy in the long run, have a huge impact on the quality of your learning and make you much more confident about the whole study process.

? How does it look from here?

Start by considering your present feelings about the challenges you face. When you think about the course, the different modules, ongoing assessments, practical tests, final exams ... what sort of shape does it all take in your head?

- Is there a clear end point, are there lots of shorter-term targets or is it a mixture of both?
- Does your course feel like one subject, with a straightforward development of knowledge and skills, or a collection of separate areas that need to be mastered in different ways?
- Are you using things you already know or learning everything from scratch?
- Does it feel like you have plenty of time to study everything required or are things already beginning to feel out of control?
- What's your gut instinct about your chances of success?

Be honest about how all these issues sit with you at the moment. This snapshot of your thoughts and feelings will help you to start analysing exactly what the challenge entails and to work out how you're going to use your memory skills to meet it.

● Break it down

It's important to focus on exactly what you're facing. Your initial, instinctive picture can quickly change when you look at it in more detail. Some students start by feeling generally good about their studies, vaguely aware of where they are in the process and pretty confident about pulling it all together when it counts – only to get a shock when they realise exactly what's in store. Others begin by feeling disorganised and unfocused but suddenly realise that there's a much clearer way forward than they thought and see how they can achieve their goals. Whether you're one of these or somewhere in between, it's vital to get the true picture of what's required, so that you can use your memory to the full. If you're over-confident or feeling defeated already or just not sure about what you need to do, you'll miss out on all the rich benefits that your memory has to offer.

So it's time to ask some important questions and to do everything you can to get the answers.

- *How will the success of your study be gauged?* What types of monitoring and assessment are involved? Are you studying purely for interest and self-development, setting your own goals for how much you want to improve – or is this a course with assessments imposed on you: marked coursework, termly quizzes, practical tests, a portfolio of evidence to be collected, end-of-year or final exams?

- *What's the timescale?* Is all your study building up to a single test or set of exams at some point in the future? Are there interim assessments to be ready for? What about the deadlines on pieces of coursework or a final folder of work? Are there some assessments that you *can't* put in the diary: unscheduled evaluations, surprise tests?

- *What sorts of things will be tested?* Consider the balance of knowledge and skills that you'll be required to show off. Will you be writing, demonstrating or discussing? Are small details important, like facts, figures, names and dates, or do you need to learn larger structures of essays, patterns of travel, broad sweeps of history? Will the facts be essential and specific – you need to know particular things to get the marks – or used at your discretion as part of longer answers? How much will you be tested on your recall and how much on your ability to do something *with* the information that's given to you on the day – analysing it, experimenting with it, comparing it with something else?

- *How will the assessments work in practice?* Will you be performing under time pressure – on paper, in a lab, in front of a panel, at a computer – or delivering a collection of work on a particular day? Will you have any choice about the challenges you tackle? Are there penalties for wrong responses or just rewards for the right ones? Will you be given any formulae, systems or maps to work from or will they need to be memorised? Find out about any written material you'll be able to take in with you – maybe a course text, reference guide, even some of your own notes – and what you'll have to store in your memory.

● *How will the result be worked out?* Do you need to impress your tutor or an external marker? How are the marks spread over different elements of your course – maybe shared between exams and coursework tasks – and are certain areas given a particularly high 'weighting' of marks?

These are just some of the questions you need to ask yourself as you start drawing up your strategy for study. In short, you're deciding how you're going to use your memory, on particular days and throughout the course. You have to be very clear about what to memorise, how you'll want to access the information and what you'll be asked to do with it. You also need to plan for all the ways that your memory skills can help. Using the techniques explained in this book you'll be able to hold everything in your head, whether it's details or larger designs, single facts or complex lists, words or numbers, essential answers or

? What do you know?

To help you plan your time and effort, you need to focus on exactly where you are now on the learning journey. You've thought about what you'll need to know at key moments during your course, so how much of that do you know now and how much more is there to come? Maybe you're reaching the end of the teaching and learning phase, so you've collected most of the information – from lectures, tutorials, demonstrations, essays, books – and you're ready to refresh the memories. Perhaps you're midway through your course, with quite a few files and folders of notes and experience of some of the knowledge and skills – but you know you'll be gathering much more. Whatever stage you're at, you've amassed a certain amount of material – even if it's from previous studies – but there's always more to be learnt. Even the final revision stage should include more research, more thinking, more refining of ideas and techniques. So plot your current position on the journey towards your final goal, thinking carefully about all the information you've already got hold of and everything you still need to get.

original thoughts and ideas. You'll feel confident about retaining all the vital information, but you'll also remember what to *do* with it: how to write about it, test it, make it, drive it, cook it – whatever skills and abilities will get you the results you want. You'll see how every aspect of your studies can be boosted by your trained and trusted memory.

Make the most of memory

As you develop a range of memory techniques, take every opportunity to use them *during* your course, not just at the end (see Chapter 14). Too many people keep memory in the closet until the 'revision' period, and then try to force it to hold everything they need for an exam. Throughout this book you'll see how memory strategies should underpin everything you do: listening to lectures, watching demonstrations, taking part in tutorials, going on visits, practising, reading, writing, thinking ... Memory must be woven into all your study, helping you to collect information, explore it, communicate it, use it – not just recall it when the exam comes around.

● Work backwards

After considering where you are now, look ahead: to the end of the course and the final goal for this stage of your studies. Everything you'll do from here on in has to work towards this target. With your memory under your control you can tailor your learning – but only if you know exactly what's required. There are plenty of ways to find out and it's important that you use as many as you can. Assessment requirements change regularly, so you certainly need official details; but you'll also benefit from talking to 'real people' and getting the inside story first-hand. Be on the lookout for any information that doesn't tally, keep checking the facts and build up the richest possible picture of the challenge that lies ahead.

- Read ... the syllabus, the exam board's guidelines, the course handbook. Highlight key details: the scope of the exam, the rules, the marking system. Read between the lines and be on the lookout for any clues about this year's test.

- Talk to ... tutors, fellow students, people who took the course last year. Remember that things change, so check the facts, but also make the most of real experiences – and the tips and strategies that no exam board is going to reveal. Don't rely on rumours about what's going to come up or be left off, but also don't miss the chance to use trusted advice to guide your planning.

● Check … past papers, revision guides, practice exams. Make sure you know what your assessment is going to look like, how it will work, what you definitely need to know - and what might be particularly useful to memorise.

Together, these strands of research should give you a detailed understanding of the learning you need to do, ready to make your memory do all the right things. They might also make you reassess where you are in your studies. Is there more work to be done, are there different areas to cover, extra skills to master? What exactly will you need from your *memory*, to give yourself the best chance of success?

✔ **Value and interest**

This strategic approach automatically boosts your memory. It alerts you to the most important aspects of the course, tags them as valuable and worthy of your attention and that immediately gives them more staying-power in your brain.

● Your grand plan

You should now be ready to create a study strategy to work from: the framework that will direct the way you use your memory skills. You can tweak it as you go along, but invest time and care from the start because it's going to guide your studies from this point on. You might make one plan for each subject you're studying or find a way to make all your challenges fit on one sheet. The important thing is that your planning shows you how to direct your memory and master everything that's asked of you.

You need to record the details physically, on paper or virtually in an electronic file, but exactly how you do that is up to you. It's a good idea to draft the plan roughly first and then shape it into a neat, final version. Follow the instructions below but adapt them to match your own needs and to reflect the style of presentation that suits you best.

Step 1: Knowledge
Make a list or diagram of all the things you want to know, if you're

going to do well. Write down headings and subheadings rather than detailed notes, but be as specific as possible about each area that has to be covered. Think carefully about the assessment requirements, but also about what you would hope to bring to this study challenge. Write it all down in black or blue.

Step 2: Skills

Now add to this collection all the skills you're studying. For your assessment, what will you need to *do*? List the skills, as specifically as you can, using a different colour from your knowledge notes – but not red, orange or green. These might be practical skills – from the fields of manufacturing, computer programming, sport – or more abstract techniques, like how to organise a poem or compare two paintings. Some skills will be specified in the syllabus or course handbook, but are there others that would help you to achieve a great result? As well as practising them, you're going to learn how to *memorise* these skills just as effectively as any other information.

Step 3: Traffic-lighting

Now it's time to prioritise all this information, ranking its importance to your ultimate success. Don't be distracted by what's most interesting or easy or by how much you think you can already remember something. You're looking for what's going to make most difference to your final results. Using all the thinking and research you've done about the challenge ahead, concentrate first on the absolutely essential areas of knowledge and skill and underline, highlight or re-colour these red, for urgent. Next, spot anything on your plan that's moderately important, but not essential. You could still perform well without this, but you'd be a lot happier and get a much better mark if you knew it well. Colour this amber or orange. Then everything else should be useful, good for putting other facts

Adding value

This traffic-lighting approach will help you to direct your time and effort, but don't think that anything coloured green is dispensable. Something that isn't *essential*, according to the syllabus, may actually be the fact or quote or brilliant idea that gets you the top grade. It makes good sense to learn the core information and cover the required elements carefully. Not knowing those will cause problems, but there are plenty of other things that *you* can decide to learn, then recall and use in the exam to brilliant effect.

and ideas into context, perhaps worth some extra marks for added detail and colour, but the least important information on the sheet – and this can be coded green.

> **i Levels of learning**
>
> As well as the breadth of learning, the *depth* is a vital aspect of study strategy. Creating this visual plan will help you to see which aspects of your course need to be learned and remembered in great depth and which require a more general, 'surface' approach. A chemical formula or quotation isn't much good if even one detail is wrong, but you don't need to learn every word of a science essay or know every one of Shakespeare's plays. What you do need is a combination of 'depths' in your rich, multi-layered learning: the formulae in the essay, the quotations in the presentation. It's whole-brain thinking at its best (see Chapter 3). Successful study combines *deep learning* and *surface learning* and this book will help you to work flexibly between the two. Recognising the required depth is vital to deciding on the particular memory technique to use; and, increasingly, *strategic learning* will become a key part of your overall studying style.

● Target your memory

When you've finished this process of noting and then traffic-lighting everything you hope to learn, spend time analysing how your memory skills are going to help.

Start a second paper list or computer file – the companion to your colour-coded plan –recording the different aspects of memory that will play their part in your success. You'll discover many more applications for your memory as you work through this book, but you've already seen how the key strategies let you gather information effectively, in whatever form it's offered, and then create lasting memories of individual words, abstract ideas and lists of any kind. So read through your plan and jot down ways in which your memory could be a major advantage.

Memory tools

Think about the key terms you'll memorise, the complex vocabulary or scientific jargon you'll master, the key concepts you'll be able to explore and connect with others, the information that can be broken down into lists and then learnt and remembered with confidence ... Could you memorise every essay you've written as a series of subheadings? Maybe you'll use your memory to learn practical skills and rehearse them in your imagination or to store everything you'll need to say in an oral exam. Perhaps you've already realised that memory skills will help you to organise your thinking, boost your confidence to choose the hardest questions or write the most creative answers.

List all the ways in which memory could strengthen your studies and improve your results, for specific areas of knowledge and skill or in terms of your overall performance – and then keep adding ideas as you learn more about what your amazing memory can do.

● Build on the foundations

Throughout this strategising stage, and in all your study, it's important to use everything you've learnt previously – to make it the foundation layer for all future learning. It's always easier to remember new things when they slot into a familiar context and you might be surprised at just how much prior knowledge you have, even in areas that you haven't studied for years.

Use your detailed, colour-coded list to help you analyse each topic in turn. How much of your past learning is still accessible today? It's a common sense strategy, but one that's often overlooked. There's no point re-learning information that's already strong – but it's also easy to assume you know something when, if you're honest, it's not at all secure in your mind.

✔ Investigating memories

You can use techniques developed by the police to help you 'interrogate' your memory and get a more accurate picture of what you already know.

- Eye witnesses are often encouraged to focus on one particular detail and see what connections it sparks – making use of the interlinked structure of memory. So, analysing your knowledge of French cuisine, you might pick a single ingredient or flavour and let your mind go from there. It's a particularly good way to get going. One thought quickly leads to another and soon the Roman tunic you started with might have opened up mental pathways to many different items of ancient clothing or the image of an oxbow lake reminded you of many more things about river formation than you thought you knew.

- Sometimes witnesses find they can remember more when they mentally re-create the conditions in which they saw something. See if it works for you. When you last studied the Russian Revolution, heard a Beethoven symphony or mended a carburettor, where were you, what was the weather like, how were you feeling?

- A third tactic is to 'play it backwards': to visualise the learning experience or even the information itself in reverse. Picture yourself at the end of a physics experiment. What happened just before you took the final temperature reading ... and before that? Go backwards through the themes discussed in last month's politics lecture, the programming sequence you were shown years ago, the cake recipe you knew in childhood and see if it helps to unearth more stored memories – with more dimensions and richer details than you might otherwise have recalled.

● Chart your progress

As you put your memory into action and gradually master every item on your plan, keep a record of your improvement. Again, how you do it is up to you. If you're working electronically, maybe you just add smiley faces to represent your changing level of confidence about each topic. A frown can turn to a grin when you've learnt something securely. If it's easy to photocopy your sheet, make yourself several versions that you can keep writing or doodling on as you update your plan. You might prefer stickers, adhesive notes, more colours ... just do whatever works, but make sure your system clearly tracks the progress of your learning and reflects the increasing part that creative memory strategies are playing in your study success.

Practical tips for strategic study

Recognise that your study has to have a *strategy*. At its best, studying is founded on interest, enjoyment, creativity and deep understanding and can offer real and important applications; but it must always be underpinned by a clear plan of action, with conscious strategies for exploiting the full power of your memory.

Plan to use your memory throughout your course, not just in the run-up to a test or exam (see Chapter 14). Memory techniques will help you to gather and organise all the information you need, to explore and expand it, as well as to recall and apply it when the time comes.

Consciously activate all your prior knowledge and skill before you memorise anything new. A mixture of imagination and logic will help you explore your existing store of memories and turn them into strong foundations for all the learning to come.

GO And now ...

6.1 **Set out your grand plan, listing the different sorts of knowledge and skills you'll need.** Start to record all the memory techniques you're going to build into your studies.

6.2 **Celebrate every forward step in your study.** Make sure you record it all on your plan. You're going to memorise everything you need to know – and charting your progress will help to keep your motivation strong.

6.3 **Use your powers of visualisation to create a 'future memory' of your success.** Imagine how it would feel to know everything on your study plan and 'see' yourself in action, achieving all your goals, using your memory skills to recall and apply all your learning with confidence and style (see Chapter 14).

LEARN TO
REMEMBER

7 | Making memories

Introduction

It's time to start practising the conscious, controlled memory-making that will take your studies to the next level. It doesn't matter what it is you need to learn. This chapter explores the core skills involved in taking hold of any kind of information and changing it in your imagination so that it suits your memory.

Key topics
- Changing study information to make it memorable
- Benefits of using 'whole-brained' study techniques
- The memory-boosting power of scenes and stories
- Tips for increasing your vocabulary
- How to remember foreign languages

Key terms
Active learning; left-/right-brain thinking; memory scenes; definitions; 'bridging' images

● Transform your learning

When you know how to use your memory, anything can be made powerfully memorable. No matter how much information there is to learn, or how abstract, complex, confusing or boring it seems to be at first glance, you can change it – into something that suits your brain and activates your memory.

Too many students waste far too much time trying to learn material in its toughest possible form, when there's a much easier, more enjoyable and infinitely more effective approach. It requires effort, but the work you put in quickly pays off. The whole experience of studying is improved as you take charge of the memory process. It's *active learning* at its very best.

✔ Both brains again

This sort of focused, strategic learning makes the most of left-brained thinking – but combines it with right-brained imagery, emotions and creativity to set up a powerful overall approach. Your original material may be logical and factual, extremely serious and very real and it's important that you can return it to that state at the end of the process, when you write it up or talk about it or use it to pass an exam. But while you're gathering and exploring and storing it in your memory, that same information needs to become imaginative, strange, colourful, funny, surprising, emotional ... and everything else that helps you to engage with it and remember it brilliantly.

✔ Trust your memory

Some people worry that creating new versions of study material just makes it harder to remember. Don't you just end up with more stuff to learn? Wouldn't it be easier to learn the information as it is? The answer is that the images, scenes and stories you invent *are* the original information, just put into a more memorable form. It's the memory process in action – and it works because it taps into the way your *brain* works. It's not more information: it's the same information, just *made memorable*.

● Making a scene

Sometimes you'll need to write long, involved memory stories to hold on to the things you need to know: detailed lists, expert presentations, complex essays (see Chapter 8). But there's also plenty of useful information that can be learned as a simple scene: just a few ideas turned into images and linked together. You may still find that you're thinking about things happening before or after, but essentially these are self-contained memory moments. All the qualities of great stories still apply, the events need to have impact and clarity and activate your memory, but you don't have to worry about a long chain of connections. With a bit of practice, the key details can be visualised and linked together in one powerful, punchy scene.

For example, here are three scientific definitions, along with ideas for mental scenes that might help you remember them. Of course, as a science student you'd also need to understand exactly what they meant, but the tips below will still come in handy as memory-joggers for terms that always seem to slip your mind. Thinking in pictures also helps you to see links with other ideas, to put you in a relaxed, imaginative frame of mind and to file information in your brain in creative and flexible ways.

For each definition there are two elements to the memory you're trying to make: the scientific term and its meaning. Your challenge is to create a memorable scene that will join these two parts together and fix them in your mind.

You'll need to make the most of the thinking skills you've warmed up: concentration, organisation, visualisation and imagination. Focus your mind, set up your strategy, picture the information and turn it into a moment that you'll remember.

Double bond: *When one atom is bonded to another by two sets of electron pairs.*

Get ready to imagine a hero being threatened by giant robotic fruit. In your mental scene, what if James Bond's stunt double, *double bond*, was faced with two atomic bombs, *two atoms*, which had been put together by two sets of electronic pears: *electron pairs*. See how powerfully you can imagine the moment: the action on screen, the soundtrack, your feelings as you watch. Picture two groups of robot pears pushing atom bombs together, while 'Double Bond' tries to work out what to do to save the day ...

Exothermic: *A reaction that gives off heat to the environment.*

Maybe you tag all your 'ex-' words with eggs in some way, so *exothermic* might suggest *eggs on a Thermos flask* or *eggs in a thermal vest*. Sometimes the process of unpicking words reminds you – usefully – of their real meaning and sometimes it takes you to imagery that has no real connection with them at all, but it still makes the memory more powerful. It always forces you to look at technical words carefully, to make the most of any prior knowledge, then find an effective way to fix the facts in your mind. For this one, bring your senses into play as you imagine the intense heat thrown out by your egg-topped Thermos or egg-filled thermal vest.

Quantum: *Something that comes in discrete units.*

Perhaps your 'con tum' – your fake stomach – comes apart in bits. What if the *Queen's tom-toms* did the same? Have fun playing around with technical words until they suggest memorable ideas, then picture a scene that connects your new version to the real meaning. Trust your brain to juggle fact and fiction. You'll find your memory is remarkably efficient and accurate when it comes to converting the bizarre imagery back to conventional scientific terms.

> ✔ **Just do it**
>
> As well as reading these examples, make sure you really do bring the pictures to life in your mind's eye. This new, active approach to learning means doing more than just reading something. You invest a few seconds in visualising it, adding senses and emotions, telling a quick story about what's just happened and what might come next, and building a whole-brained memory that should still be there when you need it.

This scene-writing technique works for definitions in any subject. It's also a good way to slot in extra details.

In economics, a 'natural monopoly' occurs when it's simply more efficient for one firm to serve an entire market.

If you wanted to remember that the water industry is a good example of this, you could build this idea into the scene you create. You might picture a Monopoly boardgame made entirely out of *natural* materials, printed in the colours of *nature*, played by *naturists* … with every property on the board being owned by a single water company. You could imagine you and your friends passing the Monopoly money between you efficiently and playing this version of the game as if it made perfect sense. In your memory, the key elements of the scene – *natural, monopoly, efficient, one firm, water company* – should tell you everything you need to know.

Have a go yourself. Here are two more definitions from economics. Create images to represent the technical terms and their definitions and then turn them into the most memorable scenes imaginable.

Wage drift: **the difference between basic pay and total earnings – including things like overtime payments, bonuses and performance-related pay.**

Bear: **an investor who thinks the price of a security (a share, for example) is going to fall.**

● Increase your wordpower

Whatever course you're taking, it's useful to be able to learn unusual words. In some subjects the technical terminology is vital and you need to know it all to understand the questions and do what it takes to score points with your answers, but in all types of study you can improve the quality of your work and impress everyone who samples it by dropping in appropriate words and phrases from your repertoire. Memory skills can help you widen your vocabulary and access it with accuracy and confidence.

Whenever you come across words that might be useful later on, take a moment to lodge them in your memory. Experiment with the look and sound of each word and explore all the associations it has for you – until the all-important images emerge. Those can then be linked to the real definition in a memorable way.

Here are some rare and specialised English words and their meanings. The first two have ideas attached to get you started. After practising with those, see how you get on learning the rest, designing your own memory scenes packed with the key information – and then testing yourself to see if they work.

buccula: a double chin
This sounds like 'book cooler'. You could picture someone keeping books cool in the folds of their chin. Imagine touching them to check this strange, fleshy book cooler is working.

chiliad: a period of one thousand years
Perhaps you break this word into two to get 'chilli ad': a TV advertisement for hot, spicy chilli that makes your mouth water and your temperature rise and goes on and on and on ... for a thousand years.

labrose: having large or thick lips

logorrhoea: excessive talking

tricorne: a hat with three points

warison: a musical note used to signal the start of an attack

Time to learn

As you experiment with this style of learning, consider how long it takes to create your memory scenes. Written down, the explanations can make them seem time-consuming; but in practice they should happen quickly. Often you can use your immediate associations for a word or idea as the basis for your imagery, then strengthen the memory after that: talking it over in your head, adding details, thinking up cleverer clues. When you're really confident with your learning skills you'll be able to transform a few bits of information into memorable pictures and punchy scenes in seconds.

Question everything

An inquisitive spirit can have a positive impact on your memory. It gets you looking at all the learning possibilities and finding new ways to engage with information. The specific questions you ask can bring you into particularly close connection with your subject matter. Questions are a simple but powerful way to strengthen the memory scenes and stories you create. You should already be exaggerating all the details, making them unusual and memorable, so it makes sense to ask yourself *why* something is so big, *what's* made it act so oddly, *how* it would look from another angle ... The connections in a scene or links within a longer story will be infinitely stronger if you've asked: *What must have just happened? Where is that going to end up? Why are these here? What's going to come next? What will this do to that ...?*

● Learning languages

Memory scenes are perfect for storing the meanings of words in other languages. Invent a 'bridging' image, based on how the foreign word looks or sounds, then think up a memorable way to link it to the real definition.

- Bring the scene to life in your imagination.
- Emphasise the important details.
- Activate your senses.
- Focus on any emotions that will trigger your recall.
- Ask questions about everything you see.

In German, *Birne* means 'pear'. It sounds like 'burner', so you could use the bridging image of a Bunsen burner, ask yourself what it's heating, wonder what that strange, sweet smell could be, then focus your mental movie camera on the juicy pear that's being burned. Exaggerate the size of the fruit, the heat of the flame, your worry as it catches fire and starts rolling towards you... Think about any extra memory clues you could add. Maybe the Bunsen burner in this scene is also shaped like a pear or you imagine the metal tube protruding from the top of the piece of fruit. Finally ask yourself exactly what you can see in your scene and what it reminds you of.

Look both ways

Get used to interrogating your language links in both 'directions'. To get the most out of them in your studies you'll need to know the definition from the foreign word and vice versa. Questions will help you to see the scene both ways. *What's on top of the Bunsen burner? What's caused that damage to the pear?*

In French, the word for wolf is *loup*. Remember the key steps: concentrate, choose your strategy, find an image, connect it to the meaning – and do anything else you can think of to enrich the memory. Put yourself in the action, engaging with it via your senses and responding to it with strong emotions.

Maybe a vicious wolf is stalking you, moving around you menacingly in a *loop*. Perhaps a wolf is piloting a stunt plane and performing *loop-the-loops* above the crowd. How can you emphasise that the animal in your mental scene is a wolf? You could do a wolf whistle to scare him off or celebrate his aeronautics or picture him dressed as Little Red Riding Hood's grandmother.

Animate the scene in your mind's eye and put yourself in the thick of the action. Use your right brain to the full to create images that are strange and funny and richly imaginative ... but also use left-brained logic to pin down the details and emphasise exactly what this memory means. Check it works both ways. Does 'wolf' trigger images of loops *and* 'le loup' take your brain straight to the wolf?

The Spanish word for eyelid is *párpado*. Once you might have looked at it on your word list, repeated it a few times, tried to use it when you could, but probably not done anything specific to fix it into your memory. Now, you know exactly what to do.

You could invent a character, 'Papa Dough', who loves kneading the dough with his eyelids. Maybe you imagine *parping* your horn at a *doe*, a female deer, which has just run in front of your car. No wonder she didn't see you: her eyelids are tightly closed. If you're a golf fan, you might come up with a tiny 'par pad': the notebook in which you record every hole you par, then fasten it to your eyelid for safekeeping.

✔ Picture clues

The images you invent need to jog your memory, but they don't have to echo every single detail of the original information. They're clues - prompts to help you retrace the mental pathways and make the right connections. Sometimes just one syllable of a word will suggest a picture that reminds you of the whole thing. In some cases, just the initial letter would be enough to trigger the whole word, so any image beginning with that letter would do the trick. You're taking control of your learning. It's up to you to decide how detailed your memory images need to be.

See how confident you are now at making information memorable. Use the foreign language definitions below to practise this new active approach to study. You're not just hoping your memory works: you're *making* it work, spending the time it takes to learn a new idea once and for all.

German

Das Hemd: shirt
Der Kiefer: jaw
Das Becken: basin

French

La carte: map
Merci: thank you
Blanc: white

Spanish

El horno: oven
El raton: mouse
La cartera: wallet

● Perfect pairs

Being able to connect just two ideas can make a huge difference in many areas of study. It's not just words and their meanings. Look carefully and you'll spot plenty of other opportunities to use this key memory skill.

For example, here are five inventors and their inventions. You might need to know these for a particular exam essay or group presentation or *choose* to remember them to help you structure your research or simply to refer to throughout your course. They could just as easily be authors and their most significant works, tutors and their specialist subjects, friends and their halls of residence ...

Christopher Cockerell (UK) – hovercraft
Edwin Beard Budding (UK) – lawnmower
Mary Anderson (USA) – windscreen wiper blade
Gerhard Fischer (Germany) – hand-held metal detector
Anastase Dragomir (Romania) – ejection seat

Why not start by connecting each inventor's surname to their famous invention? In each case you'll need to use your imagination to turn a name into a picture: something it sounds like, looks like, reminds you of. Then link that picture to the appropriate invention, creating one of your memorable story-scenes to fix it in your mind.

To get you started, maybe a *cockerel* (Cockerell) is piloting a hovercraft. Imagine watching speeded-up film of flowers *budding* (Budding) – until they're chopped to pieces by a lawnmower. Notice the windscreen wiper blade fastened *under* the *sun* (Anderson) ...

Next, you could add the inventors' first names into the mix. The cockerel could be wearing a St Christopher's medallion (Christopher). What if the *Head's winning beard* (Edwin Beard) was also cut by the lawnmower? Try to imagine your Aunt *Mary* operating the wiper blade or a *mare* being wiped by it or a couple dodging the blade while they get *married* (Mary).

The initial two-idea scene can easily hold more details and start to tell a longer story. If the medallion-wearing, hovercraft-driving cockerel was flying a union jack from the top of his vessel, you'd remember this inventor came from the UK. So did Budding – so maybe his flower horror story is happening in a quintessentially English country garden. John Wayne is marrying Marilyn Monroe next to the huge wiper blade under the sun ... so Mary Anderson must have come from the USA.

Use these stories - or better ones you think up yourself - to learn about the first three inventors, then see how confident you are to tackle the other two on your own.

? New dimensions

Think about what this rich, multi-dimensional approach to memory could mean for your studies. Information is represented with carefully chosen pictures, which are then moulded into memorable scenes with interesting stories to tell. They attract your attention, excite your senses, tap into your emotions and give you easy access to all the important details. The original material is fixed in your mind in a new, memorable form, but the true meaning is still clear. So, which parts of your course would suit this treatment? Are there technical terms, definitions, foreign words and phrases that you could start learning in this powerful way? You'd need to invest a bit of time and effort in making the memories - but what if it meant that all the key facts were at your fingertips?

🔧 Practical tips for making memories

Try to incorporate as many senses and emotions as you can into your memory scenes. Use tastes, smells, sounds and textures to strengthen the visual images in your mind and exaggerate the emotions you might be feeling if this thing was happening for real.

When you picture your scene, where do you look with your mind's eye? Think about where exactly the memory appears in your imagination and use this bit of mental geography as another clue to help you retrieve the information when you need it.

Focus on the important details of the memory you've made. Zoom in with your mental movie camera. You may have a strong scene in your mind and a good overall sense of what it's about, but which are the bits that will tell you exactly what you need to know?

7.1 Practise connecting words and their meanings. Develop powerful memory scenes that include both 'halves' of the information. Collect unusual words, vocabulary useful for a particular subject or field or terms you've been confused about in the past. Set yourself a target: to make, say, three more of these memories every day.

7.2 Start using active memory techniques to store foreign language words. Turn each word into a picture based on how it looks or sounds, then connect that with the real meaning. Could you add a particular detail to remind you about the gender of a word, if necessary: for example, seeing all masculine words in black and white and all feminine words in colour or imagining one category happening in the daytime and the other at night?

7.3 Whenever your studies involve two connected ideas – a name and a discovery, a country and a product, an organ and a disease – make a conscious decision to connect them in your mind. Go through the key steps, turn them into representative images, then activate your imagination to create a scene that's engaging, outstanding and unforgettable.

8 | Telling stories

Introduction

Stories are powerful tools for boosting memories. The best stories inspire the all-important imagery that your memory loves: they're engaging, imaginative and unusual, but they're also carefully organised and structured, so they bring together both sides of the brain. This chapter explains how any kind of information can be turned into a story and learnt in a way that's easy, enjoyable and extremely effective – whatever the focus of your studies.

Key topics

- The long tradition of learning through stories
- A step-by-step guide to memorable storytelling
- How to bring simple lists to life
- Strengthening the sequence of a memory story
- Tips for making any kind of information memorable

Key terms
Memory stories; the oral tradition; picture cues; surrealism; transitions

● Story-telling

For thousands of years, all over the world, stories have been used to enhance memory. Stories are wonderful examples of whole-brained thinking, combining logical, left-brained structure with very right-brained imagery, imagination and interest. The tradition of story-telling has served students well since ancient times and the good news is that it can be updated and made to work for your very specific study needs today.

Good stories are easy to remember, so it makes sense to start telling stories about the things you want to know. You learn to extract imagery from anything you're studying, then those images can be structured into individual scenes to help you memorise a few key ideas or woven into longer stories that store vast amounts of information.

> ### The oral tradition
>
> Before language was ever written down, spoken stories were used to keep knowledge alive. Important information was passed on by word of mouth, and oral storytelling allowed history, geography, law, myths and more to be handed down from generation to generation. To work, the stories had to be memorable, so they were told in a particular way, the performers using tried and tested techniques to fix the details in the minds of their audience. Good storytelling was very much good *memory-making*, using strong images, connections with the senses, emotional triggers, humour, excitement – anything that would make the subject matter memorable, all held in place by the solid structures of the stories themselves.

When you learn how the most memorable stories are made, and start telling some of your own, you're well on the way to remembering anything.

● Stories to remember

To invent a successful memory story you need to use the four key skills explored in Chapter 5: concentrating, visualising, organising and imagining.

- Concentrate on the task, making a conscious decision to control the memory process.
- Visualise the ideas you need to know, turning them into memorable images in your mind's eye. Even abstract concepts can be given representative picture clues.
- Organise the imagery so that it's in the easiest shape to remember: the most helpful arrangement to turn into a story.
- Imagine ... the most engaging story you can, bringing the images to life in your mind. Include senses and feelings. Ask questions

at every stage. Exaggerate everything and create a story that's colourful, funny, strange and exciting, but also organised and controlled - and now holds all your original information in a deeply memorable form.

● To-do lists

Have a go at turning the following information into a richly memorable story. It's a list of all the items you've been told to take with you to college. You *could* just write it down, but memorising it will help you to think it through, find efficient ways to go about getting hold of all these things and make sure the information is in easy reach as you walk round the shops or check your bags. It's also great brain training, because this learning technique can be used throughout your studies. With practice you'll find that anything can be learned as a story.

- Calculator
- Exam certificates
- Pinboard
- Diary
- Folders
- Dictionary
- Discount travel cards
- Desk lamp
- Bank account details
- Passport photos

✔ Get creative

As you start thinking about the best pictures to represent these things, you can immediately leave reality behind. It doesn't have to be your calculator or even a real calculator. It could be the most expensive, gold-plated calculator, hand-made for royalty; or perhaps the world's biggest calculator, suitable only for a giant's pocket. The dictionary could be Samuel Johnson's original, dusty draft. The desk lamp might be as powerful as a lighthouse. Make the information memorable right from the start - and get yourself into the best state of mind for creative thinking and learning.

When you've got some strong images in mind you can arrange them in the most helpful way. Look for any ideas that would be easy to connect. Are there any patterns in the pictures already? Where would the best starting point be – and is there something on the list that would give you a memorable place to end? Some lists need to be learnt in a particular order, but this one doesn't, so you can rearrange these images to suit your creative ideas.

The pinboard might be a good story start – and not just a normal pinboard, but one that's the size of a billboard, ready to help you remember all the other things you need to bring. What happens next is up to you. Your story will be a mixture of descriptions, actions, events: any sequence of ideas that you can narrate in your head and see in your imagination.

You could pin something to the huge pinboard straight away: an old dictionary, say, creating a shelf strong enough to hold the desk lamp. You might notice that the bright light from the lamp reflects nicely off the shiny golden calculator. Instead of numbers, what if each button on the calculator is a passport photograph of you? You could peel one off and stick it on your discount travel card – then watch as the card really does start travelling, racing round the room and making sounds like a train or bus …

That's the first six items given images and linked into an imaginative story. The giant pinboard had a dictionary fastened to it, with a lamp perched on top, which shone onto the calculator, which was covered with passport pictures. You put a picture on your travel card, which then went off on travels of its own.

See if you can now put pictures to the remaining four items and use them to continue the story. Keep asking yourself: what might happen next? What could *this* do? How would I react if I saw *those* do that to *them* …? When you've finished, go back through the story in your memory and see which bits stand out well and which need to be strengthened. Can you now say all ten things on the list from memory?

As well as learning lists of objects you can easily put people into a story. Knowing a set of names could help you write an exam essay about kings and queens, legal history or famous fashion designers; give you useful headings for a presentation on key figures in world politics; or just make you feel more confident socially as you get to know the other students on your course.

The following list is a good challenge because, this time, the order is important. As well as knowing the US presidents since the Second World War, it would be extremely useful to remember them in the right order, since they represent many important aspects of American cultural history.

The first ten US presidents since the Second World War were ...

Truman, Eisenhower, Kennedy, Johnson, Nixon, Ford, Carter, Reagan, Bush, Clinton

You can always form your pictures from a combination of real associations and completely made-up clues. In this case, you might have a very clear image of Ronald Reagan in your head, but struggle to 'see' President Eisenhower. You probably know more about Kennedy than about Truman, but even a name you've never heard before can be given a very strong picture to represent it and form the basis for a successful story.

Based on nothing more than the way these names look or sound, your images might be:

**Truman: a 'true man', testifying in court and swearing an oath
Eisenhower: an 'ice shower', freezing cold, guaranteed to wake you up
Kennedy: Ken, Barbie's plastic boyfriend
Johnson: Magic Johnson the basketball star
Nixon: an expensive Nikkon camera
Ford: an old Ford car
Carter: someone pulling a cart
Reagan: a ray gun
Bush: a large, leafy bush
Clinton: Clint Eastwood**

There are plenty of great ideas here for a memorable story. The 'true man' might be testifying while standing in an ice shower, using a Ken doll to scrub his back ...

Use that as the start of a memory story, or invent your own, and see how you get on learning all ten presidents.

- Make it as funny, violent, messy and surreal as possible.
- Enrich it with senses: the icy water in the shower, the sci-fi sound of the ray gun ...
- Think how the characters involved would feel at each stage.
- Try to put yourself in the thick of the action whenever you can.

Then check that your story works, giving you access to ten names in perfect, historically accurate order.

Transitions

When memory performers use stories to learn hundreds or even thousands of pieces of information, they pay particular attention to the transitions: the links between items. The story is a strong chain of events and huge lists can be memorised as the mind moves accurately from one thing to another, the story structure triggering each new idea. So the transitions need to be specific, clear, varied, appropriate – and memorable in themselves.

- One thing can be replaced by the next, transform into it, explode to release it.

- Items can be side by side, one on top of the other, smashed together, joined with glue.

- People, animals and objects can talk, kiss, punch or shoot each other.

Sometimes the transition will be more like a camera move or cinematic effect as the story zooms in on a particular detail, follows one thing and then picks out another or dissolves into a flashback.

Often you can choose the transition without even looking at the next idea on the list. Questions always help.

- 'What will I find if I open the box and look inside?'

- 'She's changing into another character: who?'

- 'This thing's spinning round, so what's it going to hit?'

- 'This looks fat enough to burst, showering the room with ...'

Practise inventing memorable transitions to learn the following list. It's a collection of countries, chosen and ordered according to statistics about their health-care spending. You might need to refer to this list in an exam, talk about these countries in a presentation or use the ten nations as memory-jogging headings for a detailed essay about international health policies.

US

Norway

Switzerland

Luxembourg

Canada

Netherlands

Austria

France

Belgium

Germany

However real the information you're given, and however pressing the need to know it, the best picture clues are still imaginative and fun. Choose a vivid image to represent each country, based on real associations or completely creative ideas. The United States could be a cowboy. For Norway you might watch a large rat 'gnaw away' at something – maybe the hole-covered cheese you use to stand for Switzerland … Pick images that are clear, varied and engaging and make sure that they all trigger the name of one particular country in your brain.

Then, let the storytelling begin! Maybe the cowboy keeps his pet rat in the brim of his stetson, where it gnaws away at a piece of Swiss cheese – before climbing into luxury pyjamas and getting into a luxury bed (luxury for Luxembourg), which fits into a battered old tin can (Canada). Unfortunately a giant wearing wooden clogs (from the Netherlands) steps on the can and crushes it flat, then it's picked up in the beak of an ostrich (Austria) …

Use these ideas if you want or invent your own images and transitions, but see how confidently you can create a story that will hold all ten countries and keep them in the right order. See how it feels to use both sides of your brain together: right-brained imaginative thinking, creating colourful pictures and weird and wonderful events, combined with left-brained logical sequence and order.

When you're ready, try recalling all ten countries, in order, using this powerful study technique that's been used by successful learners for centuries.

● Stories about anything

You can invent memory stories to learn a wide variety of lists and sets. In maths, maybe you need to remember the following three definitions – and then make sure you mention them all in an essay or talk.

An *ordinal number* describes a position within an ordered set, like first, second, ninety-eighth ...

A *sector* is the region within a circle bounded by two radii and one of the arcs they cut off.

A *trapezium* is a four-sided, two-dimensional shape with only one pair of parallel sides.

You might invent a bossy character called 'Orderin' Al' (*ordinal*) ordering people to stand in line: 'You're first, you go second, you're third ...!' Maybe one of the people he's bossing gets angry and comes at him with some sharp secateurs (*sector*), but only cuts a pie-slice-shaped hole in Al's shirt, before escaping on a flying trapeze (*trapezium*), landing safely in a net that just happens to have four sides, only two of them parallel ...

A story like this is a rich collection of information: images referring to maths terms, surrounded by details explaining their meanings, all engineered into a creative, connected, memorable story. In your imagination you can inject it with senses and emotions, use your 'mental movie camera' to follow the action and pick out key details and rehearse it a couple of times until it's all fixed firmly in place.

In a literature course, it might be useful to remember all the 'parts of speech': verbs, nouns, pronouns, adverbs, adjectives, prepositions, conjunctions and interjections.

See how quickly you can now give each of these eight words an image clue (maybe based on a rhyming word, one syllable or even just the first couple of letters) and put them into a story.

> ## ✔ All your own work
>
> Remember: this is your story, no one else ever needs to hear it, so free your mind, let go of your inhibitions, exaggerate all the associations that come to mind and create a personal, powerful, memorable experience. You're not trying to *find* the story, as if there's a logical 'right answer'. You're inventing it from scratch, creating a new version of the original eight words: an unforgettable story that follows no logic other than the chain of events dreamt up by you.

● Put it to the test

To finish this chapter, here's one more set of study information to help you gauge your memory confidence – and to make you an instant expert in the chronology of Shakespeare's plays.

Scholars believe that the *Henry VI* plays came first, followed by *Richard III*, *The Comedy of Errors*, *Titus Andronicus*, *The Taming of the Shrew*, *Two Gentlemen of Verona*, *Love's Labours Lost*, *Romeo and Juliet and Richard II*, with *A Midsummer Night's Dream* rounding off the first ten parts of the cannon.

Using only your imagination to think up pictures and weave them into a story, see whether you now have the active memory skills required to study and learn this list.

> ## ❓ Liberated learning
>
> Consider how it feels to be absorbing real, meaningful material in this surreal, subversive way. Once you know the chronology of these great works, you can make interesting comparisons between plays, understand more about Shakespeare's writing career, see themes emerging ... so it's an extremely useful list to learn, helping to structure the rest of your studies and give you access to vital facts. But the original information sits in your brain in a very different form:

►

a more robust memory than ever before, but changed completely. This sort of learning can be a leap of faith, so be aware of any nagging doubts you have - and try to silence them by putting this approach into practice. Look for immediate applications for your new memory skills that will prove they work and bring real benefits to your study. If you can switch on your learning like this whenever you want, which aspects of your current course could you transform into stories that engage all your thinking skills and activate your memory?

Practical tips for learning with stories

Start with pictures: carefully chosen images to represent the information you're studying. Don't just think about the story, see it happening. Exaggerate all the details, bring the pictures to life in your imagination and check that you can replay all the action vividly and accurately in your mind's eye.

Think carefully about the sequence of events that keeps everything organised in your head. Visualise clear transitions, as one thing affects the next, turns into it, fastens onto it, bursts out of it ... Make sure your story establishes a very clear order for all the elements it contains - either to memorise a particular sequence or simply to make sure that you don't miss anything off the list.

It's OK to talk to yourself! Get used to narrating your memory stories, talking them through in your head to emphasise the details, describe the action from different angles and strengthen all the memories you've made.

(GO) And now ...

8.1 Make a practical to-do list related to your current studies: things to buy, books to borrow, pieces of work to complete. Then use everything you've learnt in the book so far to turn the list into a memorable story. Keep checking this mental record over the next few days and weeks and start using memory techniques to organise your learning and your life.

8.2 Choose a set of ideas from one of your essays, research documents, presentations or skills tests; write them out in the simplest but most specific way you can; then use active learning techniques to commit them all to memory.

8.3 Stretch your memory skills by turning abstract ideas into stories. Philosophical concepts, physics theories, literary themes ... they can all be tagged with image 'clues' to jog your recall, then turned into an engaging, absorbing adventure in memory.

9

Memory journeys

Introduction

Along with carefully constructed scenes and stories, journeys have been used to support learning since ancient times. The rules for this approach have been passed down through the centuries and they remain a powerful means of absorbing any kind of study material. Spatial learning, involving travel routes, geographical maps and journeys around buildings – real and imaginary – has a key role to play in the art of memory and these age-old ideas can easily be adapted to suit the most modern study challenges.

Key topics

- The connection between place and memory
- Artificial memory and the ancient tradition of brain-training
- How the Greeks and Romans developed spatial learning systems
- A step-by-step guide to making your own memory journeys
- Expanding the technique to include extra details
- Tips for making any kind of information vivid and memorable

Key terms

Spatial memory; artificial memory; mnemonic; Ad Herennium; memory journeys; the 'Roman room' system; loci

● Locating memories

There's a strong link between physical location and memory. Returning to a place – your first school, an old house – is likely to trigger a wide range of recollections. There are so many memory prompts: not just what you can see, but also smells, sounds, textures; the things you did and said there; and the emotions you experienced when you spent time there in the past. We become so intimately familiar with the layout of

certain locations that we can walk around them with our eyes closed –
but even places we've only visited once can seem remarkably familiar
when we return.

? Memory-joggers

Do places already help you to remember? They can have an
interesting impact on memory: for example, if you listen to music in
the car, do you ever hear a particular track and instantly remember
where you were driving when it last came on? On other occasions you
might use physical location more consciously to help you out. Maybe
you imagine yourself on a desert island to calm your nerves and
relieve your stress. Have you ever gone into a room, realised you've
completely forgotten what you came in for, then walked back to the
spot where you had the idea in the first place – and remembered
again? Maybe you've discovered that simply changing the location
of a familiar item – your kettle, say, or a pair of shoes by the door –
prompts your brain that there's something important to remember.

For thousands of years we've known that places – ones to visit
for real and ones that exist only in our imagination – can activate
our memories. The human brain has a remarkable capacity for
remembering places and connecting them to other types of
information. As well as recalling individual places and knowing how to
move around them, we're extremely good at remembering the routes
between different locations. Just as the things going on in interesting
scenes stick in our minds and we can learn long and complex stories
by following the chain of events from beginning to end, we also
remember routes and journeys with very little effort. Think about the
extent of your 'spatial memory': all the different rooms you know in
detail, the buildings you can move around with ease and the journeys
that you make from memory – to and from work, around town, to
friends' houses, walks, golf courses, delivery routes, regular holiday
trips ...

Since ancient times, skilled students have been using these familiar
routes to do some amazing things with their memories.

Artificial memory

Rather than referring to physical props and gadgets that support the memory – diaries, calendars, knotted handkerchiefs, databases, electronic organisers – the term 'artificial memory' means conscious, controlled learning, using tactics and tricks of the mind to remember more. As in the memory scenes and stories you've learnt to use, information is manipulated and changed into something that fits the way the brain works. Memory journeys are just another aspect of this approach to learning. A specific, tried-and-tested technique is used to transform study material, fixing it in your brain in a way that benefits you on many levels.

- Your whole brain is activated. You can explore the information with detailed logic and unbounded creativity.

- You can start linking it to other material, applying it in interesting new ways, communicating what you know – and understand – with a whole new degree of confidence.

- You can remember it all because you've taken control and made it memorable.

'Artificial memory' may seem a quirky modern approach to learning, but it's actually a long and noble tradition, dating back to a time when memory skills were taught, respected and celebrated as a key part of intellectual life.

Ancient origins

In Ancient Greece, memory was glorified. In Greek mythology, the goddess Mnemosyne – from whose name we get the word *mnemonic*, for a memory technique or tool – was given the high position of Mother of the Muses. We know that memory techniques were developed based on physical spaces and locations, giving students strong mental frameworks for their learning. Memory was central to *thinking* as well as learning, woven into the process of exploring big ideas and new philosophies as much as keeping history and tradition alive. It seems that the great orators of the ancient world were particularly interested in memory techniques, to help them perform their speeches – and to make sure that others remembered what they had to say.

The Romans continued to develop the art of memory and, from them, we have written records of memory training and specific learning techniques. Spatial strategies were particularly important. The rhetorician and writer Quintilian analysed the clear connection between memory and place: *'for when we return to a place after a considerable absence, we not merely recognise the place itself, but remember things that we did there, and recall the persons whom we met and even the unuttered thoughts that passed through our minds when we were there before'*. The 'Roman Room' system as it came to be known relied on this simple principle: that buildings and journeys can act as storage frameworks for unrelated information. The Romans knew that you could choose a building, or even invent one, then arrange information in the form of images in particular areas (known as *loci*), see it all clearly in your mind's eye, then rediscover all the clues when you retraced your mental steps.

Crucially, your familiar journey would maintain the original order. Cicero, one of Rome's star thinkers, writers and orators, used this effect in planning and performing his public speeches, keeping all his ideas in perfect shape. He said, simply: 'The order of the places will preserve the order of the things to be remembered.'

● Time to go home

Try out the 'Roman Room' system for yourself. It makes sense to start at home, the building with which you're most familiar – and it doesn't matter what sort of place you live in. Any kind of home can be turned into a storage framework for memories of anything.

First, spend a few moments visualising your home. Think about the possible *loci* you could use, all the different rooms, areas, corridors, outside spaces, cupboards ... and consider how you 'see' this building in your mind's eye. Do you visualise it from a particular viewpoint? Take a little time to picture it from some different angles and to get a good overall view.

Next, work out a route that will take you to ten different rooms or areas of the building in a reasonably logical order. If you were showing someone around your home, where would the tour go and what would the stopping places be? Choosing ten gives you a clear, round number of places to remember, provides you with the right amount of storage space for most situations and inserts a layer of order into all the creativity that's about to take place.

When you've chosen your ten places (which could be rooms, corridors, cupboards, gardens, balconies ...) and decided on the route from the first to the last, make the journey in your head. Visualise each of the ten stopping points, imagine standing there, then think carefully about how you get to the next. Check that the order of places makes sense and feels comfortable. It's a good idea to go through the journey in reverse, too, to make sure that you know it completely.

Then you're ready to put your journey to use, filling the ten zones with image clues that will help you to remember. As with memory scenes and stories, any kind of information can be turned into vivid images and then fixed into place around the route, but now you don't have to worry about inventing the chain of events within a scene or the unfolding action in a long story. The structure of your building does the work for you, holding the information in place in whatever order you choose. You simply retrace your steps in your mind, rediscover the images you left, then translate them back into the original study material.

For example, try out the 'home journey' you just designed by learning the following list: ten clubs and societies that you want to get more information about.

Football team

Book group

Painting society

College council

Theatre group

Chess club

Student counselling centre

Social committee

Swimming team

Ballroom dancing club

Give each item on the list a memorable image clue, then put one image into each of the ten rooms or areas in your home.

Home improvement

Use everything you've learnt about memory to fix the pictures into place. Exaggerate everything you can see – and bring in as many other senses as you can. Make the pictures funny, unusual, exciting, scary … but also make use of anything already in a room to anchor the images you want to add: a piece of furniture to hold an object or person, for example, or a TV screen to broadcast a particular scene. Bring everything to life as vividly as you can, highlighting the details that matter and imagining how you'd feel if you really did find these strange things arranged around your home.

When you've inserted all your images, go through the route one more time to check they're all still there. Use the printed list to make sure your mental storehouse is now full of the right information. Then put the system to the test. Cover the list, close your eyes, start at the first point on your journey, then go from place to place rediscovering the images you left and saying exactly what they mean.

You might start on the driveway of your house and see a football match taking place, the ball kicking up the gravel as the two teams struggle to score a goal (Item 1: Football team). Maybe the second place on the journey is the front door, which has been transformed into a giant book – and you have to open the huge cover and push a hole through the pages to get inside the house (Item 2: Book group). If the hallway was awash with brightly coloured paint, sloshing up the walls and threatening to drown you, you'd certainly remember the next line of the list (Item 3: Painting society) … and so on, from place one to place ten until you've remembered everything.

When in Rome …

Think about how you might be able to use this amazingly powerful technique in your studies. It's great for learning important lists of names, books, equipment; the key points in essays or presentations; even the stages in a process or individual parts of a complex skill. Could you use it to learn which bits of apparatus to use when, which direction to turn, which technique to show off? The strong structure of the building keeps all your information safe and the journey around it ensures you get the sequence right. Match this strategy to your needs and you'll achieve a new level of confidence, whatever you're studying to know or do.

Roman rules

An anonymous text called *Ad Herennium* gives some important advice for users of the Roman Room system.

- Make sure your *loci*, the stopping points on a journey, are spacious, uncluttered and well lit.

- Plan out your *loci* so that the distances between them are roughly the same every time.

- Variety is always an important factor in memory, so design each of your *loci* to be as different as possible from the rest.

- Give yourself 'checkpoints' along the route. The Romans used to add memorable symbols to the fifth and tenth spaces of every memory journey.

● Images for ideas

The journey system provides a very solid foundation for your studies. You can use any number of different sorts of journey - buildings, walks, driving routes, golf courses - and fill each one with vital information. Your knowledge of the real world gives you a whole range of existing frameworks onto which you can map all the new things you want to know, but you can only do that if you know how to turn some abstract ideas into vivid and memorable images.

Here's a classic example. If you'd been studying the causes of the French Revolution, you might have come up with a list of notes like this.

The clergy

The nobility

The common people

Taxation

Privileges

Enlightenment

Bankruptcy

Bad harvest

Estates General

National Assembly

This list summarises the important ideas, in a sequence that would help you to explain them on paper or in person. So ... how do you put them into pictures that are clear and real enough to fill the buildings in your mind?

The first three points are fairly straightforward. If you'd chosen to memorise this material inside the local department store, you might visualise a group of priests – for the *clergy* – going round and round in the revolving entrance doors; transform the lobby area into a luxurious stately home, to remind you of the *nobility*; then put a peasant on each step of the escalator (*common people*).

Then: *Taxation*? *Privileges*? *Enlightenment*? These are a bit harder to 'see' – but, with a bit of thought, you'll find that you have a range of associations to help you create your image clues.

Taxation could be tax bills pasted all over the perfume department; tax collectors queuing up to take money from the till; or even thousands of metal *tacks* covering the shop floor.

Privileges might make you think of 'access all areas' passes round the necks of all the highly privileged-looking people sitting in the coffee shop.

For *Enlightenment*, how about a huge spotlight illuminating the changing rooms, where all the customers – trying on light-coloured clothes – have 'idea' light bulbs hanging over their heads ...?

Have a go yourself with the last four items on the list. How might these ideas be represented in pictures that could be arranged around a department store, your bedroom, the journey to the pub? Use their real meanings, any associations they inspire, or clues taken from the way the words are spelled or pronounced to help you create the sort of precise and vivid images that would activate your memory.

● Storage solutions

The journey system works best when there's one powerful picture dominating each of the *loci*, but there's room for more. Further ideas and extra details can be added to the main images, turning each place along the route into a rich, interconnected memory store. This is an essential strategy for many students with large amounts of complex information to learn. The key images store and organise the most important ideas, but the additional pictures give access to the details you need to show your true knowledge, understanding and skill.

In France, the clergy was known as the First Estate; so how about putting an estate car, with a large number 1 on the side, into one of the spaces in the department store's revolving door?

To remember that the football team trains at Friday lunchtime, you could give each of the players on your driveway a *frying* pan.

To finish this chapter, see if you can insert a main image *and* a few extra pictures into all the *loci* of a brand new memory journey.

Pick another building you're familiar with: perhaps a building on campus, the local sports centre or at a favourite holiday destination. As before, choose your ten *loci*, design and rehearse the route from the first to the last, then use this empty memory framework to memorise the following study material – notes about artistic movements, their chronology and some of the artists who made them famous.

Romanticism: Turner

Realism: Millet

Impressionism: Monet, Pisarro

Post-Impressionism: van Gogh

Symbolism: Redon

Pre-Modernist sculptors: Rodin

Art Nouveau: Mucha, Klimt

Cubism: Picasso

Expressionism: Munch

Futurism: Balla

If you chose to use a sports stadium as the setting for your journey, you might start in the car park and picture characters from your favourite *romantic* movie (Romanticism) eating *tuna*, *turning* round and round or dancing like Tina *Turner* (Turner). Then you could move to the entrance gate and find it wrapped in *reels* of film, cotton or wool (Realism) and being manned by a *miller*, covered in dusty flour (Millet).

Instead, your journey might be along a familiar route to the beach. A famous *impressionist* could be impersonating celebrities on the high street (Impressionism). Maybe passers-by are throwing *money* (Monet) at him. A huge sign above his head describes his act as *BIZARRE* (Pisarro).

Challenge yourself to set up a new journey of your choice, decorate it with images that will store all the details in this list, then see how well it's worked. Can you really study 22 separate bits of information like this and remember them all in perfect order, learning consciously and strategically, combining logic and creativity – demonstrating *artificial memory* in action?

Practical tips for making memory journeys

In all the memory journeys you use, try to visualise each of the *loci* from the same viewpoint every time. It's one less thing to think about when you need to re-create the imagery and access the original information and it gives you an increasing familiarity with the storage framework in your mind.

Talk to yourself as you set up the images and when you're reclaiming them later. Ask questions to jog your memory. Where would be the strangest place in this room to put the fish? What am I going to find behind that door? Why is there the smell of wine in this cupboard?

When you've finished with a particular set of information, 'clean out' the images so that you can use the same journey framework again. Take a walk through the *loci*, visualise all the details you added being removed and see all the spaces empty again, ready to provide the structure for your next study challenge.

GO And now ...

9.1 On paper or in a computer file start a collection of notes about the long-term journeys you set up. List the main images and extra details and summarise the real information involved. At exam time, before an important tutorial or in the lead-up to a big presentation (see Chapter 15), re-reading your notes will give you a short cut to the stored information. You'll only have to rehearse it, not start from scratch.

9.2 Use more of the places you know - real and fictional - to help you design new mental routes, ready to use throughout your studies. Even buildings in TV shows, location maps at the front of novels and videogame landscapes can provide the basis for effective memory journeys.

9.3 Design one memory route specifically to hold shopping lists. Use it whenever you think of something to buy - whether it's an item to add to the weekly grocery order or a piece of equipment to help with your studies. Just using and re-using this very practical route regularly will speed up your image-making, reinforce the connections between places and memories and keep all your learning skills sharp.

TAKE IT ALL IN

10

Re-learning to read

Introduction

Much of the information you study comes in the form of the written word – so your ability to read it effectively is a vital stage in remembering it. Learn to read well and you'll save time, access all the right material, understand it more deeply, know how to use it brilliantly – and be able to keep it fixed firmly in your memory.

Key topics

- The flexible reading skills at the heart of study
- Developing the right attitudes to reading and learning
- How to prime your brain to read and remember
- Different types of reading for different study needs
- Choosing the appropriate level of detail to learn
- Combining reading strategies with powerful memory skills

Key terms
Reading lists; visual learning; curiosity; selective reading; priming; motivation; context; previewing; active reading; SQ3R

● Take it as read

Reading is a big part of almost every kind of study. Even before a course begins you're likely to be given a reading list and this often forms the central structure of all the teaching and learning that follows. Some subjects focus on a few core texts, others require you to become familiar with a wide range of books and documents, but all demand that you can access a variety of general ideas and specific information from the printed page and electronic screen. It's not just the material you need to read for your particular course, there's all the paperwork from your place of study, there are government forms, legal documents for leases and loans ... so much that needs to be read, understood, learnt and applied with accuracy and confidence. It's tempting to think that there's just too much to remember; but, if you do it properly, reading should support your memory, while your memory skills make reading more efficient, effective and enjoyable than ever before.

Your need to read

Think about the role that reading plays in your studies and how you feel about it.

- What's your reading list like? Are you expected to read certain books before you start or to keep dipping into key texts throughout your studies or to be able to cope with extra books, documents or websites issued as the course goes on?
- How much of what you're going to read will you actually need to remember: the big themes or the small details; the author's ideas, their writing skills or the cold, hard facts they explain; generic information that's available in a range of forms or particular points from very specific books?
- Do you enjoy the reading you have to do, feel good about it, use it to access and learn the things you need or is it frustrating, time-consuming, inefficient – and certainly *not* your idea of fun?

Your approach to reading has a huge impact on what you can do with your memory and so on your whole study success. It's possible to waste huge amounts of time reading: reading the wrong things, understanding very little, remembering nothing at all. On the other hand, when you know how, you can read in a way that puts you in

Visual learning

Some students are visual learners by nature, preferring to take in information from the things they read and see. If your favourite way to find out how to use a new phone would be to read the instruction manual or online guide, you're inclined to visual learning, so you need to make the most of it in your studies, as well as strengthening other ways of accessing information – by hearing and doing. If visual learning is not your preferred style, this chapter will show you how to boost your confidence and get more out of everything that meets your eyes.

control of your learning, brings you into close contact with all the vital information and gets it into your brain in a form that you can remember easily and use to great effect.

Curiosity

One of the most important attitudes to adopt when you're reading is curiosity. You need an open, questioning approach even before you've read a word, because you should be asking yourself what the best strategy might be, which books could give you the information you need, how you'll know if they're any good, what they could offer for other parts of the course ... You should be excited about the possibilities, ready to be educated and entertained and intrigued about what you're going to discover – because all these emotions boost your memory. But you should also be ready to change tack, reject a book, take a different approach: always interested in the memory process, always questioning whether or not this particular bit of work is paying off.

● Be selective

You need to know what to read. It sounds simple, but it's absolutely essential to studying well and using your memory at its best and a lack of selectivity has been the downfall of far too many students. It's all too easy to waste time reading things that don't add anything to your learning or are pitched at the wrong level to help or just repeat information you already know. Using your memory well requires conscious, strategic effort (see Chapter 6), which starts with the choices you make about the printed resources you're going to use.

Your tutors may make most of your choices for you, especially if the course is built around a particular manual or study guide or a clearly defined set of topic texts. But even then you need to think about which bits to read when, in how much detail and if there are other publications that might strengthen your knowledge and skill and take your study forward. Your choices for further reading can make all the difference to how much you get out of your course and how impressive you're able to be in an exam.

On the other hand, some courses offer limitless possibilities. The reading list may give suggestions, but it's up to you to choose from a huge range of possible books, magazines and online materials. You know more has been written about your subject than you could read in a lifetime, so it's about focusing on the best things to read: the ones that will offer you the most benefits for the time and effort you put in.

● Priming your mind

Once you've chosen a book, there's work to do before you start to read it. You'll increase your chances of remembering the information inside if you can prepare your brain for what it's about to receive.

Motivation

Motivation boosts memory and motivation relies a great deal on the importance you give to a task – and on your expectation of it bringing success. So you can do your memory a big favour right at the start by thinking about why you've chosen a particular text. Emphasise the potential benefits. Celebrate the fact that you've found a useful publication and you're going to explore it effectively – which will improve your understanding, add to your store of information, increase your confidence to communicate and apply it and improve your results in the final exam.

Context

Use the blurb on the back cover, online reviews, reading list notes, recommendations from friends – anything that helps you to understand what this book is about and how it relates to your studies. Memory loves connections and reading is infinitely more effective if you can link new information to the things you already know. If you're studying European history and you know that the book you've borrowed is about the French Revolution, written by an author with a particular slant on events, written chronologically but with more emphasis on certain topics ... then you're ready to connect what you read now with the information you've already absorbed, to strengthen some ideas, maybe add a few new thoughts and continue the learning process rather than start something new.

Advance warning

The more you can prepare your memory for the task ahead, the better. It helps to know how challenging a text is going to be, how it's organised, the writing style, tone of voice and typical approach of the author. Again, even some simple research can make a big difference. You'll still be curious about what it contains, but you won't waste mental effort working out what to make of the content or coping with big surprises. Sometimes you'll read short, simply worded texts; at other times, much longer and more complex material; and knowing which *this* book is, in advance, is a vital part of getting the most out of it.

Previewing

Before you start reading in any detail, survey the whole book. Read the contents, the glossary, the chapter summaries. Skim-read to give yourself a general sense of the book. It's much easier to remember when you recognise something, rather than studying ideas that you're seeing for the first time. Try to create a sense of familiarity with the book, its structure and contents, before you start reading and remembering it. As well as latching on to the details it contains, your brain needs a strong sense of the 'big picture', the overall work.

Strategy

You need to know what you hope to get out of a book. Why exactly are you investing time and energy in reading it? What level of information do you hope to memorise from it? How will it help your studies – in the short and long terms – and how could it connect to other areas of your work? Answering those questions should help you set up your strategy. You should begin a book with a fairly clear idea of how long you're going to devote to it, how much detail you need to extract and which specific memory techniques will help you to succeed.

● Active reading

Memory relies on attention. An energetic, organised, positive approach allows you to absorb remarkable amounts of information – so the way you read must also be focused and active and appropriate to the task at hand.

Think about the different types of reading involved in your current studies.

- How much do you read to get a general sense of the subject and how much is about extracting specific details?
- Is everything you read 'new' material or does some of it offer familiar ideas from new directions?
- Are you aware when you're accessing information for the first time and when you're strengthening things you already know?
- How much do you change your approach to reading and learning depending on the material in front of you?

Be honest: do you have a range of subtle skills or is reading *reading*, whatever the text?

It's crucial that you know what you're going to do while you read: with your eyes, your brain, your hands ... and all the preparation you put in should guide you to the best approach.

Thinking

Sometimes your focus will be thinking: asking questions of what you read, considering how it fits in with your existing knowledge and understanding, maybe stretching your ideas and challenging your previous views. You'll want to remember any new theories or original thoughts, but the priority for now is exploring the text in front of you.

✓ **Notes and queries**

Even when you're reading and thinking, be ready to do a bit of writing when important ideas come up. Keep a notebook, voice recorder or personal organiser handy to store useful information to memorise in the future. There's a lot to be gained from *not* thinking about memory sometimes, just exploring your understanding and pushing your original thinking; but, when those sparkling thoughts and valuable questions pop up, keep them safe. A whole afternoon's reading might boil down to one brilliant breakthrough idea – which you'll want to store properly when you focus again on memory.

Recording

At other times the key activity will be note-taking: physically jotting down the information you want to use in future. Your understanding of the text and awareness of its benefits for your studies will help you to get the right level of detail: not just copying down everything and not missing the key details. Your notes can be individual words or useful phrases; bits copied straight from the text or your own notes *about* the text; bullet points, highlighted sections, doodles, cartoons ... whatever helps you to extract the information you'll need.

Enough is enough

When you're deciding how detailed your notes should be, imagine you could take them into the skills test or exam with you. How much information would you actually need? Would a few key words be enough, particular quotations, significant dates or names? There's no point writing out whole sentences if one word or even a few initials would do the job. The more you understand what you're reading and can connect it with everything else you know, the more streamlined your notes can be – and that will make them all the more transferable into your memory.

Memorising

Then there are the times when you're reading to remember, extracting vital information to keep in your mind – either during your course, to help with essays, tutorials, presentations (see Chapter 14) or at exam time (Chapter 15), gathering the material you want to have at your fingertips when the invigilator says the word 'Go'.

● Picture books

Images boost memory, so even if the books you're reading don't have any pictures at all, you need to create them. Get into the habit of seeing the things you're reading about, visualising memorable images of anything and everything. Sometimes it's easy – reading about a particular object, a famous person, a thrilling historical event – but often you need to stretch your imagination to turn abstract ideas into vivid pictures.

● Think how you'd illustrate the concepts in a computer presentation, TV advert or children's picture book.

● What would that amount look like or that emotion do to someone?

- Play with words and sounds to invent creative clues to remind you of the trickiest ideas.

- The pictures in your head can also be enriched with other senses and given feelings and brought to life – all while you're reading the words on the page.

When you do this sort of creative reading, you find that your concentration improves, you spot more connections and start understanding more of what you read – and doing something about it when you don't. You have a better short-term memory for the things you've just read and you're well ahead in the long-term learning process because you already have a stock of images ready to be put into stories and structures and retained for good.

● Levels of learning

Strategic, active reading of a text delivers key points to learn. All the general advice in this chapter so far then makes way for specific memory techniques, capitalising on everything you've learnt about memory-making. Big themes, clever insights, summary points, vital details: they can all be turned into memorable images and fixed into your brain in a form that will last.

So, what exactly do you need to learn in this way? The answer to that changes with every text and usually within each text, too. Using your memory well means staying alert to the exact needs, maintaining the right levels of detail and depth.

Scenes
Sometimes you'll need to remember a single main idea: probably with a few other details attached, but basically one concept, a summary of the article or document you've read. Learn it well and this idea can have a major impact on your work. The knowledge it represents will direct your future research and possibly be expanded upon as your studies continue, but it already holds essential information and shows that you've read, evaluated and understood your material. The form in which you memorise it is very similar to the memory scenes you set up earlier: a single, vivid moment, with activity and detail added to bring the big ideas to life.

For example, you might have read a book about Henry the Eighth and formed one key opinion: that his life and rule were about power. If you were studying this king in detail, you'd need to know much more about him than that, but as part of a wider study of English history, kings and queens or the history of politics, royalty and religion, this central theme would be very useful to know and use.

As you read about Henry, you'd probably form images based on his physical size, his striking clothing, the riches he amassed, his devastating decisions and unique approach to marriage ... and they'd all come together into a memorable scene.

- You might see Henry as even larger than he was in real life, towering over his people, in complete control.
- You could give him appropriate things to wear and objects to hold to represent his need to consume, to collect, to control.
- You'd bring in other senses – the sound of his voice, the texture of his opulent clothing, even the smell of one of his grand banquets.
- You'd see his infamous deeds, imagine how you'd feel if you were there at the time – and bring it all together as a concentrated memory store: the focus of your understanding about Henry the Eighth, ready to be added to in time, connected to other information and used to explore other aspects of your studies.

Stories

At other times there'll be more elements to remember and their sequence will be important to know. Learning processes, instructions and skills or chains of events, memory stories can provide the best strategy. Images you've invented while reading or note-taking can now be visualised clearly, organised imaginatively and learnt as engaging stories.

You might want to learn the order of planets in the solar system, so you could tell a story about your young *son* (Sun) feeling hot and using a *mercury* thermometer (Mercury) to test the temperature of his *veins* (Venus). Shocked by the reading, he'd fall to the ground (Earth) and you could give him a *Mars* bar to revive him ...

Maybe you're studying the digestive system and have highlighted the important organs, chemicals and processes involved.

Your notes might look something like this:

Digestion begins in the mouth: teeth, tongue, saliva, enzymes; starch

converted into sugar. Bolus to throat. Epiglottis covers windpipe: then to oesophagus and stomach ...

You could tell yourself a story about a monster – to make it even more exciting and vivid – focusing first on its huge mouth, the place where digestion begins, and focusing your mental movie camera on the sharp teeth and vast tongue. Maybe your friend *Sally* (saliva) is there, working hard to break down the food, using her pet *hens* (enzymes) to help. The monster is eating *stars* (starch) and these change before your eyes into sweet, powdery *sugar*, which pours into a huge *bowl* (bolus). A helpful *pig* called *Lottie* (epiglottis) covers the windpipe – gusty wind blowing out of it – and the bowl is carried away by *a soft goose* (oesophagus) towards the monster's churning stomach ... The process is already a story and you can add even more memorable elements, combine fact with fantasy and create a sequence of events that tells you everything you need to know about the information you read.

Journeys

For longer lists of ideas, especially where each point comes with several details and the order is important, memory journeys come into their own. You choose a familiar building or route to be your framework, check you know the stopping points – the *loci* – and how to navigate from the first to the last, then fill up the spaces with vivid image clues. You can do it while you're reading, afterwards from your notes or a bit of both. More details can be added whenever you like – which is particularly useful if you're reading several texts on the same subject – and well-constructed memory journeys will stay strong throughout your studies, holding vast amounts of information. Both sides of your thinking come together as the carefully chosen key ideas you've read are made truly memorable.

Learning about the history of London, you might need the following ideas to prompt you for a class discussion, presentation or exam essay.

- Mythology
- Prehistory
- Thames as tribal boundary
- Romans
- Anglo-Saxons
- Viking attacks

You could use your 'home' route and imagine ...

mythological creatures stalking along your driveway

a caveman sitting on your doorstep

the River Thames running through your entrance hall (maybe with sports *teams* for *Thames* floating with it) and tribesmen standing on either side

Roman soldiers *roamin'* around your living room

Anglo-Saxons with *angels' socks on* doing some cooking in your kitchen

ferocious, horned-helmet-wearing Vikings *biking* down the staircase towards you...

If your research about waterfalls had resulted in a detailed essay that got you good marks during the course, you'd want to learn it for the final exam. Your summary list of key points might start like this:

Waterfalls usually form when a river is young: channel is narrow and deep.
Erosion happens slowly on bedrock, faster downstream.
River flows quickly at the edge of the waterfall, causing whirlpools.
Sand and stone carried by the water increase the erosion capacity.
Caves can form under and behind waterfalls.

It doesn't matter where your memory journey happens, as long as you remember it's holding information about waterfalls. You could base it on the hotel you stayed in last summer and put a large waterfall out front to remind you of the subject matter: then ...

- step into the lobby and see a baby (to remind you of the young river) lying in a narrow, deep channel of water
- go up to the reception desk and notice it's being eroded – slowly on one side, where there's a model of a hotel bed (bedrock) but faster at the other end, which is covered in downy feathers (downstream)
- walk past the cloakroom where a hedge is growing (edge) and you can see water rushing around it in a whirlpool
- wait for a lift, which is full of sand and stones, eroding the floor and damaging it even more than the reception desk
- stand on the first floor landing and see that a dark cave has formed since your last visit – then stand under the entrance and behind it to take some photographs ...

Details

All these techniques give you the flexibility to learn at the level you choose. Scenes hold big themes and concepts, stories store sets of facts and sequences of points and memory journeys hold both key ideas and supporting details. Later in the book you'll learn more about inserting numbers, to help with dates, prices and formulae (see Chapters 11 and 15) and getting even more specific with spellings and quotations (Chapter 15), so spend a moment now thinking about the sort of information you'll need to include. In your studies, which details will be most important to add? Imagine how it's going to feel when you're able to read a document, choose exactly what to remember, then place every layer of information in your memory, ready to access whenever you want. What sorts of details will make the most difference to your study?

SQ3R

The strategies explored in this chapter represent an enriched version of SQ3R – the classic approach to reading and learning. It stands for Survey, Question, Read, Recall, Review and it certainly covers the main steps. But it's only when you incorporate the key memory techniques that your reading will truly support your study success. You've seen why it's so important to *survey*, how *questions* boost memory and the importance of *reading* actively. You know why you need to *review* at the end and consolidate the learning. But it's the most important stage, *recall*, that has been unpicked most fully, giving you a range of practical tools to turn everything you read into the most memorable form imaginable.

Being memorable

As you learn to read actively and remember the texts you study, think about the things that you *write*: essays, exam answers, even emails to friends and tutors. Are there lessons you can learn about writing in a clear and memorable way, so that all your ideas are well-explained and your best ideas given impact and power? Could you organise your ideas more, choose words that suggest strong images – do more to attract your reader's attention and motivate them to remember your work for the right reasons?

Practical tips for effective reading

Try to see a book from the point of view of its author. What do you think they're trying to achieve? What did they say in their proposal to the publisher? How have they researched and planned their book and why is it presented like this? The more you can engage with a book, the more you'll understand it, remember it and use it effectively in your studies. You'll be ready to do all the right things with your memory.

Whenever it's practically possible, write and draw on to the texts you read: in pencil in your own books, using sticky notes to avoid marking precious pages or on to photocopies of key pages. Use colour when you can, draw pictures, make the important ideas stand out and you'll find that you develop strong visual memories of the pages you 'customise' while you read.

As you create mental pictures to represent the key points, keep relating them back to the information on the page. You're going to be including a number of elements in many of your imagined scenes, so what exactly can you see – and what does it all mean?

GO And now ...

10.1 **Don't just decide to read something; decide** *how* **you're going to read it.** Consider which memory techniques will work best. Use everything you know about memory to learn it to the level of detail required.

10.2 **For every book, magazine article or website report you read, think of a picture that sums up its main purpose or big idea.** If you were redrawing the cover or illustrating the text, what imagery would represent its contents and reflect its significance in your studies? Doing this will help you to think about what you've got out of this reading experience and to look for connections with the other texts you study.

10.3 **While you're reading, stay alert to the quality of your learning.** Don't confuse understanding with *retaining*. Test yourself regularly. The information may make perfect sense when you look at it, but can you remember any of it when you close the book? If you can't, either switch on the strategies that will activate your memory or take a break until you can.

Introduction

As a student, plenty of important information gets into your brain through your ears. Your ability to listen and learn, in lectures, tutorials, conversations with tutors and friends and watching TV and listening to the radio, can have a major impact on your studies. Remembering information you hear can be a particular challenge – but there are plenty of things you can do to improve your chances of success. This chapter reveals how you can boost your listening skills, gather more useful information, explore it effectively and then remember and communicate it with confidence.

Key topics

- The difficulties of learning by listening
- Tips for remembering more from lectures
- Memory systems for numbers
- How numbers can strengthen your auditory memory
- Using your memory skills in tutorials
- Tips for remembering all the names you hear

Key terms
Auditory learning; active listening; the 'number rhyme' system; the 'number shape' system

● Hard to hear

You can learn a lot by listening, but it's a challenging way to study. Some of us are more inclined to auditory learning, preferring to listen to instructions rather than to read them or to have a book as an audio download rather than printed words on the page. Auditory learners can certainly use their natural talent in their studies, but even they face some particular challenges – and all of us need strategies for remembering more of the things we hear.

You read at your own pace, but you have to listen at someone else's – and, usually, you only get one chance to hear their words and remember the important ideas. You may be ready to concentrate in a lecture or group discussion, but at other times you're often unprepared for the things you hear, don't have equipment to write any of it down and struggle to make your memory work while you're doing something else. With written information you can use the page layout to help you recall what you read, go over it several times, underline key passages … but when you're listening, the study process feels much less controllable. It's all too easy for information to go in one ear and out the other.

Learning by listening

How much of your current study involves listening and how well suited are you to auditory learning? Think about the obvious situations in which you expect to hear important material, but also the other occasions when your listening skills are put to the test.

● Which scenarios work best for you and when is it particularly hard to listen and learn?

● When you're listening well, what's helping you to hear, concentrate, collect the information and remember it?

● When it's hard, when you lose key details – or even 'zone out' and miss learning opportunities completely – what was the problem?

Think about the aspects of your study that would benefit most if you could remember more of what you hear. Prepare to make the most of any natural talents you have in this area and to develop new ways to listen and learn.

● SQ3R again

The SQ3R process may be about reading, but its key ideas also apply to listening, so you can keep using many of the attitudes and skills you developed in the previous chapter.

● Survey your existing knowledge as well as getting an overall sense of what you're hearing.

- Question constantly – always such an important boost for your memory.
- Instead of reading words, read the meaning of what you're listening to, engage with it closely and *receive* it as fully as you can, becoming an active listener.
- Then see how much you can recall, testing the quality of your learning, reinforcing the memories.
- Finally, review what you've studied: the things you've learnt, how they'll help you, where you need to go from here.

The last chapter showed how to make memory strategies central to this whole process and when you're learning to listen well, that becomes more important than ever.

● Lectures

In many courses, lectures are a vital part of study. They provide you with important information, up-to-date details, new insights, and valuable opportunities to see things being demonstrated or to have complex ideas explained. Sometimes they structure the whole course and attendance is mandatory, while on other courses they may be optional extras, offered as additional support.

Used well, lectures present you with a rich source of information and a chance to think about it and explore it in your notes and responses.

✔ Wandering minds

One of the many challenging aspects of lectures is that you can think much faster than the lecturer can talk. This means that it's all too easy for your spare mental capacity to be used thinking about other things, distracting you from the task at hand. This is especially true at times when you don't need to make notes, but just listening is too passive and likely to lead to daydreams. So, get into the habit of reacting to everything you hear, consciously responding to each point. It's always easier to remember things that are about you, so talk to yourself silently about whether something is new to you or not, what your personal opinion is, how this idea might influence your work. See how well you can predict what the lecturer is going to talk about next. Think about the structure of the lecture, and decide if you would do anything differently if it was you up on the stage. Use the spare 'thinking space' to engage with what you're hearing, and start using your reactions to it to *remember* it.

You learn during the lecture and again later, from the notes you made, and the event itself becomes a useful memory.

When things don't go quite so well, lectures can be a complete waste of time. If you leave with few memories, poor notes and little chance of building on the experience in future, you might as well have stayed at home.

To get the most out of a lecture, you need to put in some effort before you arrive, put all your memory skills into action while you're listening, then continue the study process later on.

Before ...

- Always find out who's going to be giving the lecture. They've got the job for a reason, so use their title, expertise or experience to boost your motivation. Decide why you're going to be paying attention to what they have to say. If you know they're a poor communicator, put coping strategies in place early!

- Make sure you know what the lecture is going to be about. It's always helpful if you can do a bit of background research, so that at least some of what you hear is familiar and automatically more memorable. Think about what you already know so that the new ideas have some context and there's a framework to fasten them to. Focus on the bits that will be new to you, activating your curiosity to learn and drawing up some questions that you hope will be answered.

- Think about your learning needs for this particular lecture and the memory strategies that will suit them. Are you there to learn big ideas, themes, opinions; to see things being explained or demonstrated; or to pick up vital facts and figures? Will you have to make notes or can you get the details later from handouts, textbooks, the Internet? How much could you learn there and then and how much needs to be collected during the lecture and memorised at a later date?

During ...

- Check that you can hear and see everything you need to. If you can't, sort it out – otherwise what's the point of being there? Get comfortable, arrange your equipment and get ready to listen, learn and remember.

- Make notes that will help you to concentrate, to think about what you hear and to start remembering it. Write down your opinions and ideas about it as well as the information itself. Use different colours, add pictures, vary your note-taking style. Use everything you know about memory, making notes that are simple, clear and organised, but also visual, creative, engaging and memorable.

- Think in pictures, imagining the best ways to visualise the ideas you're hearing and kick-starting the process of remembering it.

- Some of your imagery will form naturally into a memory scene (see Chapter 7): a couple of key ideas, a few extra details, but essentially one 'store' of information – a red Mars bar wearing a warrior's helmet, for example, because you've just heard that Mars is the 'Red Planet' and named after the Roman god of war.

- At other times you'll find that you can tell stories with the images that appear (see Chapter 8). Your lecturer might talk about *inflation*, making you think of a balloon, then *wealth*, suggesting a very rich person being picked up by the balloon and looking extremely interested in what's going to happen next – for *interest rates* – and then waving to the Loan Arranger from your local bank who's down below him on the ground – because the next topic of the lecture is *loans* ...

- Always have a couple of memory journeys at the ready: mental frameworks based on buildings, walks or other types of route (see Chapter 9). They're empty at the start of the lecture, but by the end they can be full of imagery to remind you of the important things you heard: big ideas and specific details. In a lecture about Shakespeare's theatre you might find yourself imagining a huge globe on the pavement outside your house (the Globe Theatre), which smells of smoke (the first Globe was destroyed by fire); then walking to the postbox and discovering it's covered with photographs of boys and men (there were only male actors in Shakespeare's day) before moving to the oak tree up the road – illuminated by lights, exploding with fireworks and tangled with flying wires (because special effects were used extensively in Shakespeare's plays).

After ...

- When you get home, look back over your written notes and check that you can still understand what you wrote.

- Think about how you're going to use this work: maybe just keep it safe and look at it again before the second lecture in the series or write an essay about it, do more research for a tutorial or use it to revise for final exams.

- Attach any handouts or photocopies to your physical notes and store them appropriately ...

- but also take care of your mental notes – the images, scenes, stories and journeys you've created. It's a good idea to make a few written notes about *these* for later in the course and to survey and strengthen them for the future.

- Do something to practise your recall: writing that essay, talking about it in a discussion group, even just telling a friend what the lecture was about, from memory. Always spend a few minutes telling *yourself* what you learnt, going back through your imagery, using stories and journeys to access the information and to put all the ideas in order.

● Digital memory

Whatever course you're taking, numbers will feature somewhere in your studies: dates, prices, references, formulae. It's the sort of information that you often hear but struggle to retain. You could invent images for numbers on an ad hoc basis or you could use one of the many systems that have been devised over the centuries. Two of the more specialised strategies are explained later in the book, in the chapter about exam revision (Chapter 15), but the two here are easy-to-use techniques that are particularly good when you hear numbers you want to learn. They're classic examples of 'artificial memory', designed to turn abstract information into a different, much more memorable form, then to return it to its original state when required.

The 'number rhyme' system
You simply allocate an image to each digit (and to the number ten) based on rhyme. You save time by using the same basic image each time that number appears, but you bring it to life in your imagination and connect it with whatever the number really means. So, if your lecturer told you that there were seven billion people in the world, you might picture them all trying to crowd into heaven. A radio report says Facebook founder Mark Zuckerberg was born in 1984, so you watch him *skate* through the *door* of his computer company. If your tutor

mentioned the 63 known moons of Jupiter, you'd have *sticks* and *tree* to connect to that information: perhaps someone throwing sticks into a tree, to knock down not fruit or nuts but all the moons of Jupiter; or using sticks to climb a tree on Jupiter and then reach out and touch the moons.

The most popular number/rhymes are listed here – but you can change them if you have any better ideas.

0 hero
1 bun
2 shoe
3 tree
4 door
5 hive
6 sticks
7 heaven
8 skate
9 vine
10 hen

The 'number shape' system

This time you base your pre-prepared pictures on the shapes of the numbers. It's a popular strategy because it's easy to remember the key images, but they can all be extended, increasing your options and adding variety to the inventions of your memory.

Here are some basic number/shape ideas:

0 looks like a ball
1 is the same shape as a pencil
2 might be a swan
3 on its side suggests hills
4 looks like a boat with a sail
5 could be a hook
6 tipped forward resembles a cannon
7 could be a lamp
8 looks like a snowman
9 might make you think of a lollipop
10 could be pictured as a drum and drumstick

To remember that Julius Caesar visited Britain in AD55 you could visualise him being lowered into the country by two *hooks* – 5 and 5 – one under each arm.

If you heard in a lecture that the US military budget rose by 4 per cent last year, you might picture all the soldiers, tanks and guns lined up on the deck of a *sailing boat*.

Absolute zero, your tutor tells you, is equivalent to −273 degrees Celsius: that's a *swan* shining a *light* on to a *hill*, to work out why the grass is frozen solid and far too cold to eat ...

Have a go yourself. How could you use this system to remember:

- the date of the first powered flight: 1903
- the time of tomorrow's lecture: 9.45
- the number of sovereign states in Africa: 54

Practice will make you familiar with the key images, but you can also increase the possibilities. Rather than just a ball, 0 could be anything to do with sport; 1 starts as a pencil but could easily be a pen, paintbrush, piece of paper, pot of ink; 3 could be anything in the countryside; 4 every person, item, action or adjective linked to the sea. The key images become 'headings' for a large group of possible pictures.

The price of a new laptop - £487 - could be a sailor (4) throwing snowballs (8) at a lamppost (7); a submarine (4) hitting the iceberg (8) next to the lighthouse (7); or a water-filled (4) freezer (8) full of matches (7).

The first ten digits of Pi are 3.141592653. That could be a hillwalker (3) happily sketching (1) a seascape (4), then painting (1) a crane (5) - when suddenly his lollipop (9) falls out of his mouth and is eaten by an eagle (2) carrying a gun (6). So he uses a hook (5) to search through the long grass (3) ...

See what you'd do with the following facts:

- structure of DNA modelled by Crick and Watson: 1953
- number of books in the King James Bible: 66
- gestation period of an elephant: 22 months.

✔ Learning by numbers

As well as being useful for remembering important numbers, both these systems can be used to memorise lists – by numbering each item you need to know and linking it to the appropriate picture. It's a particularly effective way to remember lists you *hear*.

Hearing about these six sources of Vitamin C – blackcurrant, red pepper, parsley, orange, cauliflower, spinach – you could link them to the first six number/rhyme images:

1 (bun): blackcurrant: a delicious *bun* packed with juicy *blackcurrants*

2 (shoe): red pepper: a *red pepper* on each foot instead of a *shoe*

3 (tree): parsley: a forest of *parsley trees*

4 (door): orange: a mouldy *orange* squashed on to your front *door*

5 (hive): cauliflower: a *cauliflower* on top of the *hive*, swarming with hungry bees

6 (sticks): spinach: a cauldron of stewing *spinach*, stirred with a long *stick*.

If your lecturer tells you that the first five lectures are going to be on nutrition, exercise, sports psychology, clothing and technology physiotherapy, you might use the number/shape system to imagine ...

1: nutrition: chewing on the most nutritious pencil in the world

2: exercise: doing circuit training alongside a swan

3: sports psychology: lying on a hill to be hypnotised

4: clothing technology: wearing the latest boating gear

5: physiotherapy: using a hook instead of your injured hand.

Try it yourself. What if the next few lectures were on particular sports:

6. sprinting

7. swimming

8. golf

9. basketball

10. hockey

See how easy you find it to connect the sports to the numbers and remember them all in perfect sequence.

● Tutorials

Tutorials and small-group discussions offer great opportunities for memory improvement and for showing off your memory skills to the full.

- Take every chance you get to talk to people whose views are different from yours. See how much you really remember about a subject and how quickly you can form a robust argument, but also listen carefully to theirs and see if any of your own ideas need to change. As always, think up pictures to represent the key points being discussed, then write any extra details on to your notes when you get the chance.

- Existing mental images can easily expand or change to reflect your new information and ideas. If a fellow student talked about the two moons of Mars you could add them to your memory scene: maybe printed on to the chocolate bar's wrapper or hanging from the helmet on wires. If the tutorial made you realise that King Henry the Eighth wasn't quite as powerful as you'd thought, you could return to the memory scene you made and add a few new details: perhaps visualising cracks appearing in his palace or zooming in on his clothes to reveal damage and dirt.

- Make an effort to speak memorably: clearly, organising your ideas, using descriptive words, metaphors and stories. Do everything you can to get the others in the group thinking in pictures and offer interesting ideas to keep their attention and fire their curiosity.

● Names and faces

In tutorials you can boost your confidence, impress others with your memory skills and make the whole session run more smoothly if you know how to remember people's names. It's a practical skill that will help you throughout your time as a student – in social situations, but also within many of the subjects you study.

- When you're introduced to someone, make sure you've heard their name – otherwise how can you possibly remember it?

- Repeat the name ('Good to meet you, Shaun') and be interested in it: how's it spelt, what does it mean, where does it come from?

- Visualise the name written down. You could imagine what the person's signature might look like.

- Invent an image clue based on the name: from an association it sparks in your mind, a famous person with the same name – or something else about the way it looks or sounds. For Helen you might think of hell. The name Brian looks a lot like *brain*. Ms Beckham would probably make you think about football, and Mr MacArthur might say to you King Arthur in a plastic *mac* …

- Connect your memorable image to the real person in front of you. Use your imagination to picture Helen sprouting devilish horns and sinking through the ground into hell. Imagine looking through Brian's eyes into his throbbing brain, watching Ms Beckham head a ball or seeing Mr MacArthur pull a sword from a stone and then slide it into the pocket of his mac.

- Practise using these image clues to remember the people you meet. You can add more details as you learn them, creating rich mental scenes that supply you with other bits of useful information. Helen's using a map to find her way to hell, because she's very knowledgeable about geography. Brian's brain is stamped with shamrocks because he comes from Ireland. Learning more about your fellow students will help you to make the most of their expertise, improve your communication with them and give them another reason to remember you!

✔ Media memories

Always be ready to gather useful information from TV, film, radio, podcasts: broadcasts specifically about your studies or general information that enriches your knowledge and understanding. The more you train your memory, the more alert you'll be, able to concentrate, to recognise useful ideas and to turn them into memorable pictures that can then be fixed in your mind. Connect the images to the location you're in when you hear that particular fact or idea. A radio report about increasing tourism might prompt you to picture thousands of tourist postcards and to imagine them covering the car you're sitting in as you listen. When you're back at your desk or have a notebook to hand, cast your mind back to the place and the images – and the ideas they represent – will reappear.

Practical tips for boosting listening skills

Whatever you're listening to, think in pictures. Visualise key words in your mind's eye. Imagine the concepts being acted out in front of you. Picture powerful images appearing next to the lecturer, under your tutor's desk or on top of your digital radio.

Use memory techniques to learn the main points of a lecture. It will help you to organise your thinking, maintain your focus and establish a sound understanding. But then enrich the information later by adding more details and strengthening the memories, building on the basic mental map as your studies continue.

While you're talking to someone new, repeat their name in your head. Try to hear it in a funny voice or imagine the person themselves whispering it, singing it or shouting it loudly. To help you remember the name later, try re-creating the sounds you made in your memory.

GO **And now ...**

11.1 The next time you need to hear a set of information and learn it, number the items. Turn each number into a picture, then link each picture to the appropriate idea on the list.

11.2 Use a memory route to hold ideas for your next tutorial. Alter each image in your head as you hear other people's thoughts: either strengthening it if you still think it's true or changing it to reflect the new ideas you've heard.

11.3 Every time you watch a TV programme, listen to a news bulletin or have a conversation with friends, try to hear one thing that you could use in your work, whether it's a fact, an opinion, a question or an experience. Turn it into a powerful image to make sure you remember it in the short term, then explore it in more detail later, add it to your long-term memory store and see how soon you can put it to use in your studies.

RIGHT SHAPE, RIGHT SPACE

Getting physical

Introduction

Your physical health can have a big impact on your mental performance, particularly your memory – for good or bad. As a student it can be a real challenge to give your brain everything it needs to function effectively: the right food and drink, healthy exercise, good sleep. This chapter is full of practical advice for getting the balance right, outlining the dos and don'ts of student health and explaining how to adapt your lifestyle to help your learning and maximise your memory.

Key topics

- The connection between physical health and memory power
- How to achieve a diet that supports your study
- Brain-boosting substances and supplements
- Memory-blockers to avoid
- Benefits of exercise
- Strengthening your memory by improving your sleep

Key terms

Mens sana in corpore sano; balanced diet; food groups; Glycemic Index; omega 3 and omega 6; neurotransmitters; vitamins and minerals; herbal supplements; memory-blockers; stimulants; aerobic exercise; sleep patterns

● Feeling good

It's simple: when you're healthy and happy, your memory works better. You're free from physical and mental distractions, alert, energised, able to concentrate well, to think clearly and to make your brain do what you want. You stay in control of your learning, always organised and strategic, but you also enrich it with the creativity, the good humour and passion to achieve that makes all the difference.

A number of factors influence how well you feel. You can't control them all, but you can do everything possible to look after your body and mind and give your brain the things it needs to be brilliant.

In the words of the Roman writer Juvenal, *'mens sana in corpore sano'*. You need a healthy mind in a healthy body.

● Diet

What you eat affects your memory: over a lifetime and from moment to moment. Your diet so far has had a very direct impact on the way your physical brain has developed, but it's also influenced the way you've been able to *use* it – and that too has affected the wiring of your unique mental machine. What you eat contributes to your overall well-being and your ability to get the best from your brain at any given moment, so diet plays a significant role in determining the quality of your thinking and learning.

The best advice is pretty straightforward. Eat a balanced diet, including a wide range of good-quality, nutritious foods, as close to their natural state as possible. Just staying fit and feeling well gives your memory a major boost and a sensible diet like this ensures that your brain is getting all the key nutrients it needs. There are no magic ingredients missing from a conventionally healthy, varied diet.

? You are what you eat

Think about the quality of your diet: at its best and its worst. In the midst of student life, healthy eating can sometimes feel like a real challenge, so celebrate the times when you do manage to eat balanced meals at sensible times. But also be honest about the days or weeks when you don't eat regularly, consume too much, too little, eat too many of the wrong things and not enough of the foods that would make you feel much healthier. Think about the effects of your diet. What do you notice about your hair, skin, nails, energy levels – and, crucially, your learning – when you're eating well, compared with those times when you're definitely *not*?

Food groups

A balanced diet means eating from all the main food groups in the right sorts of proportions. On its own, no food is really 'good' or 'bad' and the balance in your diet needs to stretch beyond individual meals; but each meal does provide an opportunity to monitor the balance you're achieving and can help you get used to combining a variety of foods in sensible amounts. The ideal balance is often described in thirds: one-third starchy carbohydrates, like pasta, rice and potatoes; one-third fruit and vegetables; and one-third made up of dairy products, proteins – meat, fish, tofu, beans – and foods high in sugar and fat.

Breakfast

Your energy levels throughout the day have a big effect on your learning and the choices you make at breakfast influence how you feel long after. Breakfast *can* provide you with long-lasting fuel. It can also load you up with fat and salt and send your sugar levels through the roof, so think carefully about your first meal of the day. Slow-release carbohydrates like oats and wholegrains will keep you feeling energised and alert for much longer than high-sugar, high-fat foods. Skipping breakfast altogether has been shown to have a very detrimental effect on learning.

● Fuel your memory

Energy-giving carbohydrates make up a third of a balanced diet, while the sugars and fats that we often choose for an immediate boost should represent a much smaller part. Nurturing your memory and supporting your study means choosing your energy foods carefully. Your brain will get a temporary lift from a chocolate bar or sugary drink and that feeling of instant energy may seem to be exactly what you need – especially after a late night or hectic weekend. But a sudden rush of sugar into your bloodstream can play havoc with your concentration and confuse your thinking and you can find yourself in a negative cycle of mental highs and lows. To break the cycle, find out which foods give you the longest-lasting energy, still giving you a boost but then *keeping* you feeling alert, motivated to study well and able to use your brain at its best.

GI

The Glycemic Index measures the effects of carbohydrates on blood sugar levels. The lower a food's GI score, the more sustainable its energy is going to be, helping to keep you alert and positive and able to do all the mental work required to use your memory well. Look for opportunities to replace high-GI foods for lower-GI alternatives: maybe porridge instead of frosted cereal, wholegrain bread for white, brown rice in place of mashed potato.

● Fats

Fats are essential to the intricate levels of connectivity that make your memory so powerful. They do a number of different jobs, providing reserves of energy, adding layers of insulation to nerve cells and building the conductive connections that fire information around your brain. They're particularly important for making neurotransmitters, the chemical messengers that let neurons communicate with each other.

Getting good nutrition is always a balancing act and that's especially true in the case of fats – particularly two essential fatty acids, omega 3 and omega 6. For most of us, omega 6 is easily obtained, usually in the form of vegetable oils; but getting enough omega 3 can be more of a challenge – unless you've already seen the light and started buying oily fish or flax seed. Omega 3 fatty acids have plenty to offer your thinking and learning, boosting your speed of thought and enriching the connections within your brain. They also reduce anxiety and anger, two potential barriers to memory.

● Memory boosters

Within your varied, balanced diet, there are some substances that hold particular importance for your memory. With a bit of planning, and by changing a few buying, cooking and eating habits, it shouldn't be too hard to incorporate all of the following things into your diet.

Feeding your memory

As you read the details below, consider how well represented these substances are in your diet now and see if you need to make more of an effort to include them. If there are any obvious gaps, it might be worth looking at buying supplements, to make sure your brain is getting all the nutrition it needs.

Amino acids

Some of the amino acids absorbed from the food you eat are involved in making key neurotransmitters. *L-Glutamine*, for example, in eggs, peas, peaches and avocados, is made into the neurotransmitter GABA, which helps you to stay calm – such an important factor in study in general and memory in particular. *L-Tryptophan*, from milk, soya beans, almonds and turkey, helps to manufacture serotonin, known for its mood-lifting properties and as a weapon against depression – and so another important memory booster.

Choline

The neurotransmitter acetylcholine (see Chapter 4) seems to play a particularly important role in making and retrieving memories. As we get older, we produce less of it and a severe deficiency has been linked to dementia. Make sure you're getting enough choline in your diet, from fish, egg yolks and soya beans, as it gets converted into acetylcholine in your brain.

● Vitamins and minerals

The B complex vitamins are vital for overall health, as well as being particularly significant for your brain.

B_1: helps you to concentrate
Example sources: beans and grains

B_3/niacin: supports nerve impulses
Example sources: milk and liver

B_6: helps to manufacture the red blood cells that carry oxygen to the brain
Example sources: wholegrains, beans and fish

B_6: known to reduce irritability and boost alertness

Example sources: bananas, nuts, tuna, cauliflower and eggs

B_9/folic acid: helps the brain to get a good supply of oxygen and improves its chemical communications

Example sources: oranges, peas, broccoli, brown rice and chickpeas

B_{12}: helps to make the protective, conductive coating of neurons

Example sources: meat, cheese, eggs and fish

The antioxidant vitamins A, C and E have a good track record for improving memory. They mop up substances called free radicals, which can cause brain cell damage.

Vitamin A: helps to protect brain cell membranes from damage

Example sources: fish, egg yolks and green, leafy vegetables

Vitamin C: involved in making neurotransmitters

Example sources: oranges, kiwi fruit, cauliflower and broccoli

Vitamin E: protects cell membranes and keeps neurons healthy

Example sources: milk, eggs, nuts, olive oil and sunflower seeds

Several minerals also have a big impact on your memory.

Iron: important for good concentration

Example sources: fish, red meat, green vegetables and pulses

Calcium: strengthens the connectivity of brain cells and boosts concentration

Example sources: dairy foods, tofu and leafy green vegetables

Zinc: helps to control the communications between neurons

Example sources: meat, fish, soya beans and wholegrain bread

---

i **Herbal help**

For thousands of years people have experimented with natural memory supplements. Two substances that have become particularly well known for their brain-boosting potential are *ginkgo biloba* and *ginseng*.

The ginkgo tree from China is one of the oldest living species. For 5,000 years its leaves have been used in medications designed to improve brain function, particularly memory. The ginkgo is believed

▶

to contain compounds that cause capillaries – small blood vessels – to dilate, helping the blood to circulate in the brain.

Ginseng, in both its American and Asian forms, is another herb reputed to benefit thinking and learning. Many users report improvements in mood, mental sharpness and recall. It has been linked with increased energy and reduced stress, so has particular appeal for students.

Both of these supplements can have adverse effects when combined with other medications. If you're thinking of trying them or making any other significant changes to your diet, it's always a good idea to check with your doctor.

● Memory-blockers

As well as including all the right things in your diet, you need to be aware of the things that could be harming your memory. Some of them may well be pleasurable and the benefits to your mood and general enjoyment of life need to be weighed against their negative impact on your studies. As always, balance is the key, but be especially vigilant about the following substances.

Salt
Salt is linked to a number of health problems, including heart disease and raised blood pressure. If you have too much salt in your diet, your body can deplete itself of potassium, leading to anxiety and poor concentration: big barriers to memory.

Caffeine
There are times when this powerful stimulant seems to be just what you need to focus on your studies and, in some situations, caffeine has been shown to give a short-term boost to memory, especially for focused learning tasks. But caffeine can also reduce the overall quality of thinking and learning. It's known to lower adenosine, which helps you to relax and sleep, to raise your levels of adrenaline and to lead to the sort of distracted, jittery behaviour that does little to help your memory.

Alcohol
The impact of alcohol on the brain is complex. It changes the brain's chemistry very quickly and its effects can range from relaxation,

happy feelings and improved confidence at one end of the spectrum, to anxiety, depression and, potentially, long-term brain damage at the other. Your memory is particularly sensitive to alcohol, as too many students know to their cost. It can disrupt sleep, lower motivation, hamper decision-making and damage concentration. The pleasures of alcohol and its role in your social life need to be balanced carefully with its impact on your learning.

✔ Drugs

The brain's delicate chemical balance can quickly be changed by drugs, legal or illicit. Prescription drugs may help you to study by alleviating physical problems or improving your emotional state, but many also have a range of memory-harming side-effects, so stay alert to any problems and talk to your doctor if you're worried. There may be other options that suit you better. But the truth is that all drugs need to be treated with great caution. Aside from the risks of long-term brain damage, many of the substances that change your mental state will affect your short-term ability to use your memory as well as you could.

● Powering up, powering down

More and more studies are showing the link between physical exercise and mental performance. It makes sense: exercise is a key component of a healthy lifestyle, increasing your chances of feeling good and being motivated to learn; and physical fitness helps to supply the brain with the things it needs to work well. Aerobic exercise in particular keeps the oxygen flowing and your brain operating on top form.

Switching on for exercise should also help you to switch off: to relax and sleep, de-stressed and healthily tired. Appropriate activity and quality rest are essential parts of a lifestyle that boosts your memory and supports your study.

✔ Time for a check-up?

Don't let niggling health problems – or worries about them – get in the way of your studies. Attention and concentration are such important factors in memory and anything that's taking your mind off your work needs to be addressed. Make the most of all the health-care advice and treatment available and get yourself in the best possible shape for study.

How much good exercise do you get? Aerobic activities – like running, swimming and dancing – help the heart to pump oxygen to the brain. They also lift your mood, releasing chemicals that increase your confidence and motivation to do better at everything. Student life is busy and there are many calls on your time, but consider all the opportunities you have to stay physically fit. It's important to pick activities you enjoy and to find the forms of exercise that suit you, but they don't have to cost much money or take up too much time. Could you build more walking into your weekly routine? Are there fitness products available for your games console? How could you use exercise to widen your circle of friends, try new things and start feeling healthier, happier and more able to remember and learn?

Working hard at your studies, using your memory actively and getting plenty of exercise, you should certainly be ready for a rest. It's another challenging aspect of student life, but getting enough relaxation and sleep is essential for enjoying your studies and getting the very best results.

● Sleep

Different people need different amounts of sleep. For some of us, anything less than eight hours has a very negative impact on our well-being and alertness for the whole day, while others would feel sluggish if they got more than six. Maybe you feel better after a short nap – perhaps a few during the day – or you just have to get all your sleep in one go. Our sleep patterns change through our lives and times of illness, stress or worry can stop us sleeping, disrupt our nights or even make us need more. The key is to find the right amount of sleep to suit you, then do everything you can to get quality, regular rest. It's essential for your physical fitness and mental well-being, especially your ability to learn.

There's ongoing research into the links between sleep and memory. It seems that our mental connections can be reshaped during sleep, so it's no wonder that young children need so much more sleep than old people since they have such a wealth of new connections in their neural networks. Experiments are revealing the role of sleep in consolidating learning, especially for skills. Sleep appears to protect fresh learning from the potential interference of new information.

Sleep survey

How would you rate the quality of your sleep at the moment?

- Do you think you're getting the right amount for you?
- It's normal to be tired by night-time, but are you also suffering from fatigue during the day?
- Think about your sleep patterns over a particular week. When you don't get enough sleep, is it an issue of time – having too much to do, wanting to stay up, trying to fit in with others – or is getting to sleep and staying there a problem?
- When you don't get your proper amount of rest, do you get a chance to catch up or does the tiredness accumulate?
- Have you noticed the impact of sleep on your memory-making and recall?

Think about the times when you've felt in great shape for study and other occasions when poor sleep has caused problems. Use your experiences to decide on the sleep patterns that would be best for your memory and think carefully about what you could do to achieve them.

To get a good night's sleep, to consolidate your learning, refresh your memory skills and prepare you for optimum study the next day, do the following.

- Get plenty of exercise – but don't take it *too* close to bedtime or you'll overstimulate your system.
- Avoid heavy meals late at night or foods that hamper your digestion or give you heartburn.
- Be careful with foods that include tyramine (like bacon, cheese, nuts and soy sauce), which releases norepinephrine, stimulating the brain.
- Say no to stimulating, sugar- and caffeine-loaded drinks close to bedtime.
- If you're hungry, see if a combination of tryptophan-rich foods and carbohydrates helps to relax you for sleep: like a turkey or

peanut-butter sandwich or a bowl of wholegrain, low-sugar cereal.

- Calcium has also been linked to improved sleep, so the traditional mug of warm milk could be the perfect nightcap.

- Avoid excessive alcohol as it can make you restless, wake you up to go to the toilet during the night and increase snoring – which can restrict breathing and reduce the amount of oxygen getting to your brain.

- Improve your sleeping environment, making it calm, cool (about 18° Celsius is ideal), dark and airy.

- Set a regular time to go to bed and to wake up. Even when life gets in the way, try to get back into your routine as soon as you can.

- To relax, try some simple breathing exercises. Breathe with your abdomen, not your chest; breathe in through your nose for three seconds, out for another three; then pause for three seconds before starting again, focusing on your steady breathing and its relaxing effects.

- If you still can't drop off, try not to worry. Even four hours is enough to give you many of the benefits of sleep, so focus on relaxing rather than sleeping – or get up and do something calming until you're ready to try again.

Switching off

If stressful thoughts are stopping you sleeping – or getting in the way of your study generally – *trying* to relax can actually have the opposite effect, focusing your mind on the problem. A useful strategy is to try 'replacing' your stressful thoughts and a spot of simple reverse psychology can often do the trick. *Try not to think about a pink elephant.* Of course now it's hard *not* to think about one – and, for a while, a challenge to think about anything else; so this can be a surprisingly effective way to take your mind away from whatever was causing you worry. Your memory skills can heighten the effect. Why not tell yourself *not* to think about … lying on the warm sand of a desert island or floating in an infinity pool at a luxurious tropical spa … Think about the details, the senses and emotions that you're trying *not* to bring to mind. It isn't hard to tempt your brain to immerse itself in much more pleasant, positive and relaxing thoughts.

Practical tips for health and well-being

Drink more water. About 75 per cent of your brain is water and dehydration can have a very negative impact on thinking and memory. Sip water throughout the day and you'll avoid headaches and drowsiness and stay alert and focused for longer.

Find simple ways to build exercise into your day. Take the stairs instead of the lift. Get off the bus a couple of stops early and walk the rest of the way. Use regular exercise to improve your circulation, lift your mood – and give you extra time to think.

Develop a relaxing bedtime routine that works for you: maybe taking a bath, listening to music, reading for pleasure. Make it as regular as possible. Even brushing your teeth for the same length of time every night will help you to slip into a nightly rhythm and expect to fall asleep.

GO And now ...

12.1 **Keep a diet diary for a couple of weeks.** You might be surprised about what you're actually eating and drinking. Think carefully about the balance of your diet, look for any memory-boosting substances you're missing and see if there are any easy changes that could make big differences to your physical well-being and mental strength.

12.2 **Challenge yourself to take up a new type of exercise:** something high-energy, if that suits you, or a more gentle form that will still support your study. Even walking six to nine miles in a week has been shown to benefit the brain.

12.3 **Keep sleep separate from study.** Could you clear any of your books or equipment from your bedroom? Agree the point in the evening when you're going to stop thinking about study, so that you'll return to it the next day refreshed, motivated and ready to use your brain brilliantly.

13 | Memory zones

Introduction

Your memory skills are very sensitive to your environment. This chapter is about setting up the best possible study space, where everything supports your learning and works *with* your memory, not against it. You're going to be spending a lot of time in this place, so you'll get so much more out of your memory if the physical conditions are right – and you know how to use your learning environment to maximum effect.

Key topics

- The impact of environment on memory
- Choosing the best place to learn
- Improving the physical conditions
- How to create a 'whole-brain' memory zone
- Beating the distractions that hamper learning
- Using your learning space to get the most out of your memory

Key terms

Learning environment; left- and right-brained thinking; distractions; memory rituals; learning partners; context-dependent memory

● A place to remember

The locations in which you study can have a powerful influence on how well you get on. Your memory is affected by your mood (see Chapter 4), so the way you feel when you're sitting in a particular place has to have an impact, as do a number of physical factors: how comfortable you are, the lighting, temperature and ventilation and the level of access you have to the things you need. You need to set up your learning space so that your brain works well there; protect it so that it keeps supporting your study; and use it wisely – as one of the most significant tools in your memory kit.

? Favourite places

Before you consider your study environment, spend a moment thinking about the way places in general affect your state of mind: inside and out, old or new, carefully designed or completely natural.

- Where do you feel most relaxed, happiest?
- Which places make you feel like working hard and which make you want to switch off?
- Where are you most alert, focused, creative, ambitious?
- What sorts of locations do you find most distracting, de-motivating, depressing?

Think about why places have such an effect of the way you feel – and the way your brain works.

● Your study space

You have only so much choice about where you do your study. The trick is to do everything you can to find a suitable spot, then to improve it, to make every conceivable adjustment until it suits your memory as much as it possibly can. It's well worth the investment, in time, effort and, perhaps, a little money. As well as this place affecting how you feel about your studies, and how successfully you can use your memory, it will also become *part* of your memories, inextricably linked to everything you learn there.

✔ Personal preferences

Everything in this chapter depends on you: your character, your learning style, your likes and dislikes and your particular needs from your study space. Many great thinkers have had their own idiosyncrasies about their thinking zones: certain objects nearby, particular sounds, helpful smells. Roald Dahls' ideas came to him in a shed at the bottom of his garden, always with the same blanket over his knees. Lord Byron said he wrote better when his cat was nearby. Einstein believed that the quality of light in certain places helped him to think and Dr Yoshiro Nakamatsu, one of Japan's most creative inventors, claims his best ideas come to him at the bottom of a swimming pool. You just need to find the space that works for you.

Current conditions

Think about the place where you do most of your studying now. Maybe you're in it at this moment or you can go there in your imagination – to take a look around and consider how much it influences your work, for good or bad. Is this the only place where you consciously use your memory skills or one of several learning zones? Did you choose it or are you spending your time here by default? What aspects of this location help you to learn and which ones get in the way? Do you come here with the expectation of enjoying your study and doing it well?

Stake your territory

The place where you work needs to be *your* space – even if it's just one part of a single room. Ideally, it should be physically separate, a room that you know – and everyone else agrees – is your learning 'zone'. If that's not possible, you need to make the boundaries clear. Think about how you could personalise your space to give you a sense of ownership. You'll need study materials and equipment here, so could you use them to help structure the space? When you're working here, it must be very clear that you're doing something specific, different from the things that you and others do elsewhere. This is the place where your memory works its most powerful magic and where you need a special degree of focus.

● Physical perfection

You have to be realistic, but you also have to be ambitious about the place where you study. Use the following checklist to help you make the most of what you've got and carry out any possible improvements to your learning environment.

Lighting
To use your memory well you need to be able to see your material and to concentrate for lengthy periods without straining your eyes. Study in natural light when you can; and, when you can't, experiment with different types of lighting and varieties of bulb to find the combination that feels right for you.

Ventilation
What can you do to improve the air quality of your study space? A

good supply of oxygen is vital for staying alert, concentrating for long periods and getting the most out of your memory skills.

Temperature

If the temperature's too high, your brain will feel sluggish and sleepy. If it's too low, you'll be wasting vital energy trying to warm up. Either way, discomfort is distracting, causing you to lose your focus and pay less attention to your learning. Sort out the temperature so that you can use your memory for the right length of time - not just as long as you can last!

Furniture

Chess champions choose their competition chairs and game tables very carefully. They know they'll find it hard to concentrate well, access their memories and focus on the mental challenge facing them if their posture isn't right. It's true for you, too, so do your best to sort out the furniture and furnishings in your room. You need to be sitting comfortably, but not *too* comfortably: breathing well, able to stay in place for long enough to get the job done and within reach of everything you need to support your memory.

● Whole-brain memory zones

The best study spaces encourage both left- and right-brained thinking: the two halves that come together in powerful memory-making (see Chapter 3).

Your room needs to be organised, because your *thinking* needs to be organised (see Chapter 5). Invest time in sorting out your stuff: books, files and notes; pens, pencils and other stationery equipment; computers, cables, printers, external drives ... You need to know you have all the right learning materials and all the tools of the study trade. It's also important to have space for note-taking, writing, drawing and for all the new material you generate and gather to be filed efficiently. Your study space must have an air of organisation about it, supporting your logical thinking, prioritising, sequencing, structuring, and all the other traditionally 'left brain' skills involved in memory.

But ... a truly effective learning environment is also laid back, fun and creative. Think about the colours that inspire your ideas, the paintings, photographs and quotations that will excite your imagination. Make sure you have coloured pens for memorable note-taking, paper for doodling, objects to handle that will stimulate your free thinking. All the best memory strategies are organised and logical, but they're also driven by instinctive, imaginative, right-brained brilliance.

Remembering *why*

Find a picture, object, letter or anything else that reminds you why you're putting all this effort into your memory skills and display it prominently in your learning space. What are you going to achieve by using your memory this well? How will your life improve? Who's going to be proud of you? Give yourself some powerful, visual reminders to keep your eyes on the prize and maintain your motivation, attention and effort, even when the going gets tough.

● Defeating distractions

Your brain's susceptibility to distractions is one of the reasons why you simply don't remember more. Your in-built survival instincts redirect your mental energy towards the most urgent need, moment to moment, but that can ruin your concentration and remove your attention from what you *should* be learning.

To stay in control of your memory, you need to:

- eliminate distracting noises: background conversations, pet noises, music that stops you concentrating
- have a clear plan of action for every session spent in your study space and stick to it
- use kinaesthetic activities – desk toys, stress balls, twirling a pen, doodling – to keep your mind occupied, energised and focused on the task at hand
- limit interruptions: from visitors, mobile phones, email accounts ...

The soundtracks to study

Whether or not you listen to music while you learn is very much a matter of personal choice – as long as you're honest. Some people work best in absolute silence, others need music to relax their mind and keep them focused and the type of track that does that could be rock, pop, classical, new age ... So you need to think carefully about whether music in general helps or hinders your memory and if specific musical styles are appropriate. If you can hear lyrics clearly, your brain is likely to listen to them: trying to follow them if they're familiar or to understand them if they're not. If you do find music helps, try different genres and a range of artists until you discover the ones that improve your mood and help you to concentrate – but don't relax you too much, overstimulate you or draw your thoughts and ideas away from your work.

● Memory routines

Organise your memory zone so that it helps you to slip into easy routines. It's another way that you can strengthen your resolve and keep your mental energy focused on learning.

Having all your equipment to hand is a good start, so that you can get going straight away. The more confident you are in your memory skills, the more you'll want to work in the same effective way every time. Develop habits that get you accessing all the thinking skills involved in memory: maybe always checking the same study timetable on the wall, then always picking up the same set of coloured pens for creative doodling. Choose something symbolic that can always accompany your established routines: moving a particular object on to your desk, for example, putting on a cap, taking off your shoes. Your memory loves to follow patterns and a familiar physical routine will help you to return to the right point in the study process and – even more importantly – to re-create the same successful state of mind.

● Memory teams

There are pros and cons involved in letting others into your study space. You definitely need time on your own, devoted to focused, personal learning, but you may also find it helps to work with 'learning partners' at key points in the process. As always, the key is to experiment, to reflect and to be honest about what's working and what's not.

The *advantages* of working with others include:

- having someone to test your recall and someone you can test back in return, enriching learning and strengthening memories for both of you
- being able to discuss key points, probing your understanding and challenging you to remember your best ideas and argue them effectively
- picking up useful learning strategies from someone doing the same work as you – but maybe with different thinking styles that you can incorporate into your own approach
- using each other's help to find resources, get organised and stay motivated and focused on study.

The *disadvantages* include:

- finding it too easy to get distracted and lose track of the task at hand
- letting someone else's negative thoughts infect yours
- trying to learn at the wrong pace or level
- wasting time on learning techniques that suit one or the other of you – or neither.

Crowd control

How much do *you* get out of studying with others? Is it impossible to have anyone even near when you're trying to think and learn or do you get lonely, distracted and de-motivated without them? Is it best to put in the groundwork first, then meet up with a friend to test each other and share ideas or is it even more effective to talk first and do your focused study later? With a bit of careful planning you can balance your study time to get the support you need *and* the independent input that's essential to top-class learning. Alone or in a study 'team', the strategies explained in this book will always let you use your memory powerfully and match your learning to *you*.

● Work the room

You already know about the powerful link between place and memory (see Chapter 9) and it makes sense to use your real study space to help you learn. The memory journeys you create to hold your study information can and should be based on a wide range of familiar places, but why not build one around your working area: a structure that will act as a sort of 'emergency store' for sudden thoughts, vital extra details and any odd bits and pieces that you need to remember.

Choose ten spaces around your study area, in a sequence you'll remember. Your space might be large enough to take an actual journey, walking from the doorway to the bookcase, say, then standing by the cupboard, next to the computer, under that picture on the wall … Maybe you take a journey with your eyes, moving your gaze from the door handle to the poster, the ornament on the windowsill to the brackets under the shelf, choosing key *details* of the room rather than areas, large objects or real storage spaces.

Rehearse the route in your imagination, then use it to hold images for all the odd bits of information you have to juggle.

- If you decide you need to do more research about power stations, picture a cooling tower blocking the doorway or a tiny nuclear reactor built into the door handle.

- To remember to meet your tutor at 6 p.m., imagine there's a cannon (representing 6 in the 'number shape' system, see Chapter 11) with his picture on it firing from the top of the bookcase or emblazoned across the poster on the wall.

- You know you'll forget to mention Churchill in your essay unless you picture him hiding in the cupboard or turned into a statue on the windowsill.

Get into the habit of checking your study space route regularly: certainly every time you enter the room for real, but also at other times during the day. Invest those few seconds it takes to choose an image and fix it in place and it will still be there as a powerful reminder whenever you look back to check.

When it's served its purpose, picture that 'slot' in the route empty so that you can re-use it for another important idea.

● A change of scenery

It's important to have a main study space, where you keep the majority of your physical materials and which you adapt to suit your personal approach to learning. This is the place where you need to feel best about your memory and all the focused and creative work you do there will give it an important role within your memories themselves. When you're sitting in the exam hall and trying to remember a particular article you read or great idea you had, you'll be able to use your sense of place as a way of re-connecting with the key information. All the familiar senses and feelings you associate with your learning environment will be potential pathways ... back to the moment ... when you studied the information ... that you need to remember *now*.

The principle of *context-dependent memory* means that you're more likely to remember things in the same context – place, company, state of mind – as when you learnt them. You can make use of it in exams by taking yourself back to your study space in your imagination; but you also need to make sure that you really know your stuff *anywhere*, not just when you're sitting in a particular place. That's the beauty of the memory techniques in this book: they make use of familiar places to store information and take you back to it, but they're strong enough not to depend on context to work. When you've learnt something properly, you know it anywhere.

Get around

Having a familiar learning space is good, but it's also vital to feel comfortable using your memory elsewhere. If you only ever explore your ideas, test yourself and answer practice papers in your room, those things will feel distinctly unfamiliar when you're in the exam, however hard you try to re-create the conditions in your head. So change your scenery sometimes, find new places in which to think, work and remember. Learn to trust your memory in any environment, strengthen it by going to places that don't naturally suit; and, in the process, create a varied range of 'geographical' memories. The more memorable the places themselves the better: unusual, pleasurable, exciting, intriguing. You'd have a very good chance of remembering what you read about in Piccadilly Circus, thought about in the hot tub or learnt on the way to a first date. When you understand how memory works, everywhere you go can become a powerful place to learn.

Practical tips for improving your learning space

Make sure everyone knows where you're working and when. Talk to your housemates, put a sign on the door, send out a status update – whatever it takes for them – and you – to know that your study is officially *on*.

Use all your senses to improve your working conditions and to connect you to your study space. See which scents boost your concentration and create positive, happy thoughts. As well as music, are there other sounds that help you learn? What about the texture of objects you handle while you work or particular flavours of snacks and drinks that keep you going? Make your study space appeal to your senses – then use your senses to take you back there and remember everything you learnt.

Use your memory skills to remember where you've put things. Every time you file an important document, think logically about the route you'll need to take to find it; do some good kinaesthetic learning by exaggerating the physical movement of opening a particular drawer or talking to yourself as you choose which box to use; and switch on your imagination to superimpose a memory cue on the appropriate folder, notebook or part of the room. Pick unforgettable file names, think up funny reasons why things are where they are and use all your memory skills to stay in control of *everything* you need.

GO **And now ...**

13.1 **Use this chapter as a checklist to improve your study environment today.** Do everything you practically can to make it a great place to practise the art of memory.

13.2 **Start using a memory journey based on your work space to hold bits of information that you might otherwise forget.** Any study-related task, fact, question or idea can be turned into a memorable image and held in place until it's needed – then deleted or replaced by something new.

▶

13.3 **As part of your overall study planning, start deciding in advance where you're going to be working.** Think about why that's the right choice for a particular task – and whether or not it will help to invite someone else into your 'memory zone'. These are important factors in your success, so don't leave them to chance.

TOTAL RECALL

Student survival

Introduction

You can use your memory skills in many different areas of your student life. The chapter after this one focuses on exams and assessments, traditionally the time for memory to come into its own. But you'll achieve your full potential only if you use your trained memory throughout your course – in your studies and in everything else you do.

Key topics

- Keeping your memories fresh throughout your studies
- The importance of testing to strengthen recall
- Organising your study sessions to suit your memory
- Tips for connecting and combining different areas of your learning
- Adding new information into your memory stores
- Making memory central to your student life – even when the going gets tough

Key terms
The 'forgetting curve'; the testing effect; distributed learning; study schedules

● Staying on top

When your memory is under your control you can learn actively and effectively all the way through your course, not just when exams come around. You deserve to get the full benefit of using your brain this well – and you *need* to be learning like this all the time, because successful study is an ongoing process. You do the right things to fix memories in place, then you continue doing so to keep them there.

i Beating the curve

The nineteenth-century German psychologist Hermann Ebbinghaus did pioneering work into the way memories fade over time. He looked at different sorts of information, analysing the natural 'drop-off' in recall accuracy and exploring the factors that might make a difference. He highlighted many of the principles now firmly embedded in memory training – that understanding supports memory, for example; organising and connecting data keeps it fresh in the mind for longer; and skills-based learning is more robust than many other forms of study. But he had particular impact with his work on the 'forgetting curve': the natural weakening of memory traces as time goes by.

Memories fade, but Ebbinghaus showed that they actually strengthen for a short while after the initial learning – so the graph goes up, first, before curving down. How to fight the fade, to get the line going up again? Ebbinghaus found that short 'refreshers' spaced out over time were more effective than intensive, concentrated revision. The best way to beat the curve was to learn the information well in the first place and then to refresh the memories at well-chosen intervals, strengthening the learning while making each revision session a supportive new memory itself.

? Ups and downs

Think about the study approach you've adopted in the past. How effective *long term* has your learning been? Have you ever read an article, attended a lecture or learnt something for a mid-course test and then found that you remembered virtually nothing of it when you needed it later in the course? You may have still understood it all perfectly, but think about how your *memories* of it faded. How much time did you waste starting again from scratch? But if you've ever refreshed your learning at a time when you didn't actually need it for anything specific, did that help to get it ready for when it *was* required? What difference might it make if you started strengthening all your memories throughout your course: like a circus plate-spinner, knowing just when to go back to each plate and give it a boost and keeping them *all* going round?

● Memory-boosting

The memory 'curve' goes up for a while after a study session, so make the most of it. A short time after you've stopped for a break, your brain has consolidated its learning, so test your memory then and remind yourself of the active memorising you've done. Put the finishing touches to your memories at this high point of recall and fix them firmly in your brain. Then return to them: after a day, a week and a month. Each time, start by testing yourself (which shows you the areas to keep working on as much as it strengthens any information that does come back) then rehearse the memory techniques you used the first time around, improving the imagery, building stronger connections, maybe also adding a few new reminders into the mix. Interrogate your learning, engage fully with the process of recalling and refining your material and you'll create increasingly robust memories for the future.

Testing, testing

Different theories have emerged about why the 'testing effect' is so powerful. Some research points to the new connections that are forged each time learning is put to the test. Another view is that the testing rehearses techniques for *retrieving* the information, making those faster and sharper each time. The memory strategies in this book use both these principles.

Get into the habit of testing yourself while you're learning, then when your brain has had a chance to embed the learning and again whenever you're refreshing the information. Improve the images and links you've invented to make your memory work, add new ones, strengthen them in your mind; but also practise using them, rehearsing how each clue you've left triggers your recall. The testing effect has been shown to have particular power when the memories need to be retrieved in a week's time, so it fits very well with study – and especially with exam preparation.

Testing is good for revealing gaps and providing 'progress reports' throughout your studies, but its true role in strategic, active memory-making is so much more important than that.

Getting better

Remember, you're not starting again every time. By refreshing the memories before they've faded very far, you're building on them, enriching them, making it easier to revise them the next time you come back. When you study like this, each mini refresher doesn't just restore the memory; it strengthens it, giving you another active learning experience to draw on in future. You're strengthening the memory *strategy*, *how* you remember this information, as much as the information itself.

● Multi-layered learning

The secure structures you put in place – scenes, stories and routes filled with powerful imagery – provide the foundation for your study. You have an overall idea about the things you've learnt and what they mean, but you keep returning to the details to refresh them and to enrich them, because you're always curious, always eager to gather and understand and learn more. Your strategic approach combines these deep layers of memory with more 'surface' learning: when you skim through a new document, chat about a topic with friends, take some useful points from a TV programme. The new ideas keep you interested, remind you of key themes, refresh the long-held information – and can easily be added to the central 'core' of your learning.

Do something different

An effective and enjoyable way to test *and* strengthen your learning involves challenging yourself to do something unusual with it. Do you know your material well enough to turn it into a song? Do you understand it clearly enough to sum it up as a limerick, haiku or rap? Do you remember enough of it to write it out in the form of a quiz, turn it into a play, storyboard it as a movie, report on it for a newspaper? Use visual, auditory and kinaesthetic activities to explore and enrich your memories and to make it possible to go along several different mental pathways to get them back.

● Spread the load

Ebbinghaus investigated 'distributed learning': learning in shorter bursts spread over a longer period of time. As many studies have also shown since, it's possible to devote much less time to learning when you do it like this; although, of course, the overall learning period will be longer. So, if you need to know something quickly, you may still choose to study flat out until it's there; but if you have a wider 'window', it makes sense to learn in short, spaced sessions. There are several benefits.

- You create more 'starts' and 'ends' of study periods, so you make the most of the powerful 'primacy' and 'recency' effects (see Chapter 2).

- After each session, your brain has a chance to consolidate the learning – while you're getting on with other things.

- Each new study period starts with a test of what you still remember from the last and regular testing is a powerful way of strengthening memories.

- In shorter sessions you run less risk of getting distracted or bored.

- A longer overall period of time gives you more opportunities to gain useful, interesting, enriching information to bring in from elsewhere.

Working the system

How might these sensible tactics be applied to the way you use your memory for study? Think about how you could start organising your time and effort differently, learning particular subjects in shorter bursts but returning to them more regularly. After memorising something properly the first time, what would it feel like to refresh your strategies after an hour, a day, a month ... and then to *keep* keeping it all fresh for as long as necessary? As well as testing your recall and strengthening the memories you made the first time round, what other quick activities could you do to enrich your learning and keep all those plates spinning? It takes a bit of organising, but it's an efficient and extremely effective approach: a strategic combination of deep and surface learning styles.

How long to go on?

You need to find the length of study session that suits you. The more you get to know your memory and how to use it, the more aware you'll be of when it's working well and when it's not (see Chapter 5). You need to schedule study sessions that are long enough to explore your material in depth and to use all your memory skills, but not so long that you lose focus, get bored or feel overwhelmed by the amount of information you're processing. Changing subjects or topics within a session may be enough to kick-start your concentration and reawaken your interest, but you also need to spot the point when you're not making or retrieving memories well and your brain needs a break. It depends a lot on the type of information you're working with, the point in the study process you've reached – and on *you*.

● Shuffling the pieces

Think of your study as a jigsaw puzzle: one that you're designing and making as well as slotting together. Each piece is the memory you've created for a key bit of information. You keep going back to each piece to remind yourself about it, to improve its design, to enrich its colours, to practise using it ... and in doing so you also find the best ways to put all the pieces together. You get different areas of the overall picture to join up. Over time, the more you think about it, gather more information and share your ideas with others, the better you get at organising all the individual bits – into a structure that's intricate in detail, but overall a simple and sensible way to hold your learning in one place.

Maybe you've created memory scenes to remind you of the function of key organs in the human body. It would make sense then to connect the scenes in some way, giving you one 'place' to go in your memory but still allowing easy access to all the details. You'd find it easier to spot the similarities and differences between organs, boost your understanding, answer questions creatively ... and continually strengthen your memories.

You might have designed memory journeys to learn three different essays on Shakespeare, each one full of key ideas, character names, quotations, vocabulary, critical theories. You could then join these three pieces together, giving you one journey to remember, but with the three parts – and all the internal details – memorable and clear. You might imagine a path taking you from the last of your pet shop *loci* (the structure that held all your learning about *The Taming of the Shrew*) to the first stopping point on your Windsor Castle journey (all about *The Merry Wives of Windsor*) and then visualise a secret tunnel getting you to the fairy forest memory journey that stores everything you need to know about *A Midsummer Night's Dream*. Bringing the different journeys together would make it easier to spot recurring images, highlighting important themes and letting you pick out key information efficiently.

Maybe you have a whole range of essays on French history, to turn into one large structure and another set about Germany. Each collection would become a mass of interconnected ideas: memory scenes merged, stories lined up, journeys joined. Then the two collections could be brought close together, allowing you to make even more connections and comparisons and to navigate a huge amount of complex material. Within each learning system there might be mini-scenes reminding you about tricky foreign words, stories holding short lists of place names, people or political movements, journeys letting you reconstruct whole essays – and you'd be able to tap into it all. It would still match your memory: vivid, interesting, unusual, connected; and it would be manageable, the individual pieces all helping to hold each other together.

● Filling in the gaps

As you refresh your memories and find new ways to arrange them in your mind, you can also expand them and add more details.

When more is less

Don't worry about new information making study harder. When you've trained your memory, extra details actually make the original ideas *easier* to recall. They add colour, create new connections, arouse your interest and strengthen your core knowledge even more.

Maybe you've imagined a thermometer lying outside the post office to remind you that the nearest planet to the sun is Mercury and there's a large Venn diagram painted on the newsagent's wall next door, telling you that the next planet is Venus. These are key facts in themselves, but you can easily add more details as you obtain them.

Some of the craters on Mercury have ice in them, so why not balance some ice cubes on top of the thermometer - and have the big movie dog Beethoven licking one, to remind you that the largest crater on Mercury is called *Beethoven*. You could add cartoon illustrations to the Venn diagram representing mountains, volcanoes and sand - all features of the planet Venus.

You might have set up a memory structure to hold information about global warming. If one of your main images was a canister of methane gas, with a photograph of *me* for *methane* on the side, reminding you of one of the causes of the global warming phenomenon, you could embellish it with extra memorable details.

- Cover the canister in leaves and dirt: it's a natural cause.
- Imagine touching the canister and feeling how cold and wet it is: methane gas is released from Arctic tundra and wetlands.
- Cover the canister with a mini greenhouse: methane is a greenhouse gas.

By the end of your course you might have several connected memory journeys storing your knowledge about climate change. You could focus on the one about global warming, home in on the key image of the methane gas canister, find all the other clues in one place in your brain - the leaves, the cold, the wet, the greenhouse - and have easy access to a wide range of important ideas.

● Sort yourself out

Using your memory well means constantly improving the way your learning's organised. You spot new patterns, make clever connections and tweak the structures of your memory accordingly. This whole-brained combination of creativity and organisation can become part of your everyday student life.

Think in pictures

Visualise the plans you make for everything: social occasions, club meetings, travel arrangements … Picture the events, exaggerate the images, improve your chances of remembering them - and spot recurring ideas that might highlight potential clashes, possible economies and practical improvements to your plans. Use your improving imagination to save time and money and to feel more organised about everything.

Create a to-do room
Pick a real place you pass by several times every day and use it to hold image clues about everyday jobs. Into the virtual version of your room, building or landmark, fix images for errands, appointments, responsibilities, deadlines. Then, every time you pass the real place during the day you'll be reminded to check your mental to-do room and find the images you've left: the laundry in the doorway reminding you to pick up your dry-cleaning, the cheques glued to the ceiling prompting you to go to the bank ... It's a great way of 'remembering to remember' all those things that can save you so much time and effort if you get them right.

Learn the lingo
Becoming a student means learning a whole new language. Your memory skills will come in handy to collect new words and their meanings and gather them together in one place in your mind. Choose an appropriate location – your library, say, the student union building or common room – and insert imagery to remind you that ...

- the *proctor* is someone who monitors you during exams (while doing some *PR* work for a *doctor*, sitting there writing a medical press release?)
- a *bursary* now refers to an amount of money given as support to qualifying students (which *bursts* out of the bank in their direction?)
- a *graduand* is someone who's passed the course, but not had their graduation ceremony yet (and is getting to that *gradually* or *glad-handing* the crowd?)

... and to store a memory for every other unusual term you meet.

As well as saving time and money, making a good impression, improving your communication and boosting your confidence, all these strategies will help you to stay organised in your *mind* – and you know how vital that is for getting the most out of your memory.

● Getting it done

Your understanding of memory and the strategies you've developed can come in very handy when the going gets tough.

- You know that distractions damage memories, so, if there's a particular worry on your mind, make a conscious decision to deal with it later, at a given time, after your study session has finished. Don't try to think through a problem and use your memory well at the same time, because it simply won't work.

- When you're finding it hard to get down to work, spend a moment visualising your reasons for doing well. Develop key pictures that you can flash into your mind, reminding you about the job you're going to get, the travelling you'll do, the people you'll impress, the sense of achievement and happiness you'll enjoy ... when you succeed in your study. When a session goes particularly well, focus on the positive feelings and think up images that will remind you of them the next time your resolve is faltering.

- If things go wrong - poor grades, missed deadlines, bad tutorials - invest a bit of time working on the memories. Don't let the rest of your efforts be hampered by negative thoughts. Focus on the image that keeps coming back to you and try seeing it from a more forgiving angle. In your imagination, change the sizes of the people involved, the volume of sounds, the impact of your actions. Make the memory less worrying and distracting, but also use it to guide you positively in future. Maybe you really could see it more from someone else's viewpoint or tone down your anger or speed up your work ... not just in your re-shaped memory but also in your actual behaviour from this point on.

⚒ Practical tips for student life

As you create more and more memory images, scenes, stories, journeys ... keep a simple written record of how they fit together: a map of your structured learning. Make notes about what each bit of the 'jigsaw' reminds you of, how they all fit together and which areas relate to which parts of your study. Keep looking back at this grand plan, giving yourself a strong overall view of your growing memory store.

Every time you begin a study session, make sure you have two clear goals: one for how much information you want to cover and the other for the quality of the memories you want to create. Are you doing some surface learning, reviewing an article, listening to a radio programme, skimming through your notes or are you working on a more detailed level? You'll need to know so that you can use your memory skills appropriately and gauge how successful you've been.

Use your written notes to complement your imaginative inventions. The notes will help you form your memories, giving you details to add and patterns to follow; and your memory work may well inform your notes, making you insert new ideas or organise things differently. All the notes you make should include reminders of any memory techniques you use. They need to summarise both the study information itself and the ways you've chosen to fix it in your mind.

(GO) And now ...

14.1 Refresh something that you learned an hour ago, a day ago and a month ago. Test yourself, strengthen your memories, fill in any gaps and think of active, engaging ways to enrich your learning.

14.2 Start using your memory skills to organise your days. Don't just hope to remember that the tutorial is at 2 p.m.: imagine the swan on your tutor's head (a swan might be your image for 2 in the 'number shape' system, see Chapter 11). Don't guess that the meeting is in room 84: see the snowman sailing there ... (snowman = 8, sailing boat = 4). Save time, be more impressive, *feel* more organised.

14.3 Set up a memory room for feedback: ideas about improving your studies, from tutors, fellow students – and from your own reflections. Every time you get some useful advice, think up an image that will represent it memorably and fix it in place in your memory. Keep looking back at this store of good ideas and ways ahead and use it as a checklist for your continual improvement and increasing success.

15 | Memory for exams

Introduction

Use your memory well throughout your studies and the exams just fall into place. It's still crucial that you bring out your very best memory techniques for the tests themselves and there are some new strategies to put into action, but mostly it should feel like you're putting the finishing touches to a long-running process: the powerful learning you've been doing ever since you started your course. This chapter will show you how to use your memory skills brilliantly in the final few weeks, then during the exams themselves, helping you to access all your rich learning under pressure – and to enjoy this chance to shine.

Key topics

- Planning the final weeks of study before assessments and exams
- The practical preparations that will make your memory work when it matters most
- Refreshing all the memories you've made throughout your studies
- Adding extra details, using specific strategies for the things you need to know
- Staying in shape, coping with pressure
- Using memory skills to get you in the best frame of mind to be brilliant

Key terms

Assessments; revision; core information; additional detail; the 'word length' system; the Major System

● Putting it all together

All the memory techniques explored in this book are useful and effective in their own right. Even if you never took a test or exam in your life, by using your memory effectively you'd have learnt in an easier and more enjoyable way, deepened your understanding, had more creative ideas, organised your time better ... and developed learning skills to last a lifetime. But assessments are a reality for most students and the good news is that memory skills help at every level. All the quality learning and brain-training you do during your course puts you in the perfect place to achieve the very best results, adopting a confident approach to tests of every kind.

Keep it simple

It's tempting to switch to panic mode when exams come around, to believe the hype and to start thinking and working differently. But the key memory principles still apply and everything that's worked well in your study so far will keep working for you now. In fact, it's more important than ever that you stay in control of your learning and keep doing all the things that support it. You've put in a great deal of effort to perfect your mindset, establish good learning routines, alter your lifestyle to boost your brain, set up a great place to study and use your memory in a way that really works. Even if you've come to this book late on in the process, you'll see that the core approach is focused, strategic and controlled and realise that there's plenty still to be gained, if you keep your cool. You need to operate your memory calmly, creatively and confidently – and *use* memory skills to enhance all those positive effects and more.

The final push

Think about how assessments figure in your studies. Do you have to face written exams, take skills tests, complete assessed coursework or show off your abilities some other way? Do these challenges come throughout your course, each term or all at the end? In many courses there's a point where the lectures and tutorials stop to give way for a revision period before the big exams, so think about how long you'll get to prepare specifically, how many different subjects you'll need to work on at once and what *sort* of study you'll have to do. Will you have covered everything and just have to revise it or might there be more research for you to do on your own? Will your preparation time be spent rehearsing set skills and formulaic answers or getting ready for anything that might be thrown at you in the exam?

Get it together

At the start of any preparation period before exams, invest time in thinking through your strategy and getting together everything you need (see Chapter 6). Make sure you have access to all your notes, books and computer files, plus any new information that you need to use – or could benefit from studying now. Think through your priorities.

● Are you going over everything or just particular areas?

● How much of your time now will be spent rehearsing skills and procedures, strengthening your recall of information, practising your exam technique?

● Is this the time to work with others or alone?

● Do you need to organise particular activities to help you get ready: foreign-language conversations, field trips, museum visits, theatre nights?

Focus on the way your memory is going to be tested, think about all that you've done so far to prepare and highlight the last few things that will get you ready for the challenge ahead.

● Still on track?

Now is also the time to check the precise details of your assessments. You did this earlier to put your memory strategies in place and you should still have some notes to help, but it's important to look again and make sure you know exactly what you're doing.

Some of the most important questions are these.

● When, where and for how long will you be tested?
● Will you be able to take in anything to prompt your memory?
● What topics are definitely going be covered?
● Will there be any choices to make about questions to attempt or skills to show?
● How will these tests be marked?

It's the answers you get to these questions that will dictate how you use your memory skills in the final weeks, days, hours and minutes. They'll help you prioritise your time and effort, choose the right strategies to bring out now and help you to get there feeling relaxed, focused and confident about doing your very best.

The essentials

Decide what the absolute minimum level of knowledge and skill would be to pass the coming test. What is the core information, the absolutely essential stuff? If you got sick or had a family emergency between now and your big assessment, which memories would be enough to get you through? The traffic-light lists you made earlier should be very useful now. Think carefully about what's most important, start with that – and then, if any of those big problems do arise, you'll still stand a chance. In an emergency the core memories would be secure, helping you to reconstruct the rest.

● Revise, refresh, re-engage

In the last chapter you learnt the importance of regular refreshers, returning to the memories you've made, testing yourself, improving the learning, adding new thoughts and engaging with the information even more closely. That's exactly what has to happen now as you focus on getting *everything* back to the 'front' of your memory.

Your ongoing memory work should have put you in a great position to refresh all the information you need, quickly and enjoyably. Revising doesn't mean learning it all again: you're just strengthening each memory and practising using it brilliantly.

- Focus on a particular topic. Test your memory: can you remember the main points, the facts and figures, key vocabulary, the structure of essays, great ideas you had during your study?

- Investigate your learning strategies. What imagery have you put in place to trigger your recall? Did you set up memory scenes, stories, journeys? See what's still in place in your brain, then check all the written evidence you've left yourself about your 'artificial memories': the comments and sketches you added to your notes and the grand plans you've sketched out to show how it should all fit together.

- Think how you're going to strengthen any shaky memories or fill in specific gaps. Which imagery just isn't working? Which memory structures are not holding firm? Use what you did before as a starting point, but build on it, using your memory-making skills – focusing, visualising, organising, imagining – to shore up your learning.

- To enrich your memories further, and to prepare your brain to access them flexibly in the exams, spend some time thinking, questioning, debating and extending the main ideas. If you have time, do more research into the areas that interest you – or even dip into other topics that might give you new insights into this one.

● The devil's in the details

The run-up to exams is a good time to work on the details of your subject. This is where the strategic side of memory techniques comes into its own. Some details will be useful to retain for as long as possible, but there'll also be plenty of facts, figures, names, dates, quotations, formulae … that, if you're honest, you'd only hope to remember for the duration of the exam. They can make a big difference to your marks and demonstrate that you can learn anything and incorporate it cleverly and creatively in your answers. The details help you to get your message across and show the depth of your understanding, so it's good to know that your memory skills will let you gather as many as you want and hold on to them for just as long as you need.

● Numbers

If you find that you're adding lots of numbers to your knowledge, here are two more strategies to try. The 'number rhyme' and 'number shape' systems may continue to serve you well, but the following techniques give you more options, especially when numbers – in dates, statistics, formulae, map references and elsewhere – play a particularly important part in your studies.

The 'word length' system
You simply pick words with the appropriate letter-count for the numbers you want to memorise. You have the flexibility to choose memorable words, phrases and even whole sentences, then you use your imagination to link them with whatever the original numbers really mean.

Albert Einstein was born in 1879: a (1) creative (8) science (7) superstar (9).
An imperial pint is equal to 568ml: enjoy (5) drinks (6) sensibly (8)

The Leaning Tower of Pisa is 55.86m tall: tower (5) leans (5), tourists (8) marvel (6)

Invest some time matching words to numbers, then use everything you know about memory to fix them in your mind – as vivid, unusual, engaging images that can be inserted into the rest of your learning wherever you want. Jot them down on your written notes as well as bringing them to life in your mind's eye.

The Major System
This technique dates back to the 1600s and has been developed over the centuries since. Each digit is represented by a designated consonant or consonants and you turn these into words and phrases by including any vowels that help. Then, as with the 'word length' system, you turn your chosen words into images and attach them to the appropriate memory scenes, stories or routes.

The number code

A typical version of the Major System looks like this.

0: *s*, *z* or soft *c*: *z* is the first letter of the word zero and the other consonants here sound similar

1: *d* or *t*: like the number 1, these letters both have one downstroke

2: *n*: like 2, it has two downstrokes

3: *m*: this time both the number and its letter have three downstrokes

4: *r*: the last letter of 'four'; and 4 and R are almost mirror images

5: *l*: L is the Roman numeral for 50

6: *j*, *sh*, soft *ch*, *dg*, *zh* and soft *g*: a handwritten *j* looks like a 6 – and *g* like a 6 upside down

7: *k*, hard *c*, hard *g*, hard *ch*, *q* or *qu*: there are two 7s in a capital K

8: *f* or *v*: a handwritten *f* looks like an 8 and *v* sounds similar

9: *b* or *p*: *b* looks like 9 rotated, *p* could be a mirror-image 9 and the two letters have a similar sound

---

The Major System is phonetic, so spellings don't matter. Just use the consonant sounds of a word to create its number code.

The Battle of Waterloo was fought in 1815. The letter options for these digits include T, F, D and L, giving you the phrase TOUGH DEAL (or TuF DeaL) – and Waterloo certainly was a tough deal for Napoleon!

Leonardo da Vinci was born in 1452. This time you could use D for 1, R for 4, L for 5 and N for 2, then fill in the vowels to get DARLIN. Maybe that's what he called the model who posed for the *Mona Lisa*.

One pound is equivalent to 454 grams. Imagine weighing a ROLLER in pounds and grams: a grass roller, a high roller, a Rolls-Royce ... (The code here is RoLeR: you don't use double letters as they only make one sound).

A record-breaking Jackson Pollock painting sold for $140 million. Imagine you're there as he paints it, watching intently as the paint DRIES ...

● Words

As you prepare for exams you may find you need to work on words in more detail than normal. Here are some tips for common verbal challenges.

Spellings

Use your memory skills to do more than just hope for the best. Getting spellings right is an important way to impress in tests. Actively memorise the spellings of key words for your particular studies, or just the ones you always forget.

- Highlight any difficult details in bold colours in your mind.
- Exaggerate bits that are easy to confuse or miss, making the key letters huge, 3D, alive ... anything to make them stick out.
- Imagine you're taking a mental photograph of this vivid, highlighted word.
- Lift your paper so that you're looking up at the spellings. This matches your upwards eye-movements when you're *recalling* spellings. You may also find it easier to look up to the left – the

direction most people's eyes turn when they're remembering words.

- Project the word in your mind's eye and practise spelling it backwards.
- Write out tricky spellings several times to help build up 'muscle memories'.

Tricks and triggers ✔

Use your 'creatively organised' memory skills to do anything you can to make words memorable. Often you'll find that remembering just one detail is enough to give you the whole word.

Picture Donald Duck and Steven Spielberg living at the same *address* to remember both sets of double letters: aDDreSS.

Think about a member of the college IT team showing total *commitment* to their job and you won't add an extra *t* in the middle.

Create a *miniature* clay figure stuttering 'I ... I ... I' to remind you about the *i*.

Let Eva help you find the *relevant* paperwork.

See the stationer in his *stationery* shop.

Find engaging clues within the words themselves or invent your own, then use your imagination to make them powerfully memorable.

● Numbers *and* words

Your course may involve some specific number/word combinations, but a classic example is quotations: just the sorts of details to embed in your memory in the run-up to an exam. Think in pictures, use a system to handle the numbers, then link both elements together as a valuable memory store.

Here are three quotations from Shakespeare's *Macbeth* and ideas about how to remember them. You could easily think up a strategy of your own for any word-and-number combinations in your own work.

'There's daggers in men's smiles': Act 2, Scene 3
Think literally: picture men smiling and revealing sharp, shiny daggers where their teeth should be. Then you could imagine a GNOME stealing all the daggers and running off. In the Major System, GNOME (NoMe) gives you the digits 2 and 3: Act 2, Scene 3.

'Fair is foul, and foul is fair': Act I, Scene i
Maybe the foul is actually a fowl, a very fair fowl: a beautiful DODO.
The Major System turns DoDo into 1 and 1: Act I, Scene i.

'Out, damned spot! Out, I say!': Act V, Scene i
Why not imagine Macbeth shouting at his dog called Spot – otherwise
known as FIDO. FiDo gives you Act 5, Scene 1.

Arresting images like these – for every kind of detail you want to
learn – can easily be inserted into existing memory structures as you
continue to prepare for your exams. Keep the pictures fresh, practise
finding and using them and feel confident that they'll be at your
fingertips, ready for you to add that extra sparkle to your work.

? Be specific

Consider which extra details might benefit your learning, to boost
your accuracy, make your answers more impressive and let you dip
into your memory stores and extract the facts and figures that the
examiners want to see. Which memory strategies could you combine
to help you cope with anything? Think about the benefits to your study
of this powerful approach: organised and creative, left- and right-
brained, surface and deep learning combined.

✔ Time management

Your time is always precious, but it's especially so in the run-up to tests.
Use any 'dead' time – waiting for the bus, queuing at the till – to dip into
your memories and keep them alive. If you're feeling alert, why waste the
chance to strengthen your learning? But the opposite is also true. At times
of day when you're too tired to use your memory well, switch to more
functional tasks, like tidying, form-filling or filing.

● Pressure tests

As an assessment or exam approaches, keep the faith, keep using your
memory well, bring all the information back to the surface – and add
any details that might make a difference. Use the familiar strategies
of your study so far to maintain a sense of normality. Everything

you've done up to this point has been about increasing your memory confidence, so now's the time to let that shine through. Tell yourself that the only pressure is positive pressure and that it's coming from *you*: from the need to show off what you can do and to use your memory skills to the full. It should feel exciting that you have this final time to step everything up a notch.

- Focus on the key steps of the memory process.
- Push your imagination as far as it will go.
- Read and listen more actively than ever before.
- Keep using your trained brain to gather, explore and learn new ideas.
- Choose the right strategies to make memories about *anything*.
- Bring everything you've learnt back to mind more powerfully than ever before.

Mind gone blank?

All the memory training you've done should ensure that you can access all the right information and use it in the most effective ways, even under the pressure of an exam. But if you do find yourself struggling, try to relax, because stress will just make it worse. Give your memory time to work its magic by moving on to another question if you can. Also, try some of the 'crime-scene' strategies that help to boost eye-witnesses' memories (see Chapter 6) – even in situations more stressful than yours!

● Healthy body, healthy mind

Exams are a test of your physical endurance and mental strength – and you know now how closely the two are connected (see Chapter 12). Your target is to get to every assessment or test feeling that you're at the peak of your powers: healthy, relaxed, focused, energised, confident that your brain is in top form and all the learning you've done is within easy reach. That's why it's so important that the few weeks beforehand are *not* an exhausting, sleep-deprived, worried slog. You need to use the deadlines and the increased sense of urgency to intensify everything that's been going well throughout your course, all the things that will get you into the mental and physical shape of your life.

- **Take particular care of your physical health.** Make sure you're getting all the nutrition you need to use your brain at its best, taking enough exercise to keep the oxygen flowing and the stress at bay and having the amount of sleep that's right for you. Working late, especially just before a big test, is likely to do your memory more harm than good. After your final study session, give your brain the down-time it needs to consolidate the learning and replenish its energy for the major thinking challenge ahead.

- **Use memory skills to keep your motivation strong.** Think about the inspirational images you've invented throughout your course: powerful reminders of your reasons for working so hard and using your brain this well. Reflect on the small victories you've had along the way and on all the evidence you've amassed that your new approach to study is working. You don't have to hope your memory will work: you know how to make it work – so keep the faith. You've seen your amazing memory in action throughout your course and now it's time to show everyone else!

- **Let your trained imagination provide you with 'memories' of success.** You should now be very good at inventing vivid scenes and stories (see Chapter 8) and going on journeys in your imagination (Chapter 9). You know how to include senses and feelings and to immerse yourself in something completely imaginary (Chapters 1 and 3), so why not flash forward to the exam and rehearse your success. You're in control of this experience, so make it as useful to you as possible, accentuating all the positive feelings. Make sure you also focus on the *process* that will bring you success. Think about how you'll use memory skills to get to all the right information, use it accurately and creatively, carry out the key skills with confidence, communicate your best ideas – and do it all with memorable impact and style.

Practical tips for taking exams

Don't let other people talk you out of your positive state of mind or shake your confidence in your memory. They may well not be feeling very good, if they haven't put in the right sort of effort or prepared themselves properly. But you *have*, so you need to stay clear of their negative thoughts and resist the temptation to start doing yourself down. Keep telling yourself how *well* you're going to do - and believe it!

Because you're now so confident ... take some time out before a big memory test. If you've used your memory well throughout your course you can afford to relax more than other people and you'll actually benefit from a bit of variety. Even if it's just the odd hour here and there, make a conscious decision to do something different, fun, refreshing. You won't damage your memory: in fact, you'll do it a favour.

Just before a big test, refresh your memory one last time. Don't worry about absorbing anything new, but quickly remind yourself of your deep learning - the core material of your course - *and* the surface layers: the wide variety of facts and ideas you can access. Reinforce the richness of your memory and enjoy the way it all feels so close.

(GO) And now ...

15.1 **Plot a timeline, from where you are now to where you need to be in your studies by the time your next big memory test comes around.** Use it to plan your preparation carefully, leaving time for all the activities outlined in this chapter. Include opportunities for rest, space for the unexpected and time to enjoy putting the finishing touches to your learning.

15.2 **Don't waste any of the work you've put in so far.** Whatever you choose to revise and refresh, start with the memories you've already laid down. Test yourself, look back at the notes you've made about images and structures, explore the different ways you've stored the information - and then *build* on your learning, strengthening your memories rather than having to make them all again from scratch.

15.3 **Start the mental rehearsals early.** Think through all the ways you're going to benefit from having a trained memory. See yourself accessing your learning confidently, accurately, creatively - whatever form the assessment takes - then ... *do it*.

Further reading

Books

Baddeley, Alan (2004) *Your Memory: A user's guide*. London: Carlton Books.

Buzan, Tony (2009) *The Memory Book*. London: BBC Active.

Channon, Mark (2011) *Teach Yourself How To Remember Anything*. London: Hodder Education.

Kirton, Bill (2010) *Brilliant Study Skills*. Harlow: Pearson Education.

Lorayne, Harry, 2002. *The Complete Guide to Memory Mastery*. Hollywood, FL: Frederick Fell.

McMillan, Kathleen and Weyers, Jonathan (2010) *How to Succeed in Exams and Assessments*. Harlow: Pearson Education.

O'Brien, Dominic (2005) *How to Develop a Brilliant Memory Week by Week*. London: Duncan Baird Publishers.

Sherratt, Patrick (2009) *Passing Exams for Dummies*. Chichester, West Sussex: Wiley.

Websites

http://academictips.org

www.bbc.co.uk/sn/tvradio/programmes/memory

www.bbc.co.uk/science/humanbody/mind/surveys/memory

http://helpguide.org/life/improving_memory.htm

http://howtostudy.org

http://learningskillsfoundation.com

www.memory-improvement-tips.com/exercise.html

www.improvememory.org